D0528117

WOMEN MEAN BUSINESS

WOMEN MEAN BUSINESS

A
SUCCESS AND
SURVIVAL GUIDE
FOR THE
WOMAN EXECUTIVE

Veronica Groocock

EBURY PRESS
LONDON

Published by Ebury Press
Division of The National Magazine Company Ltd
Colquhoun House
27–37 Broadwick Street
London W1V 1FR

First impression 1988

ISBN 0 85223 667 0 (Hardback)
0 85223 672 7 (Paperback)

Editor: Fiona MacIntyre
Designer: Roger Daniels

Computerset by MFK Typesetting Ltd., Hitchin, Herts.
Printed and bound in Great Britain by Anchor Brendon, Tiptree,
Essex

An award scheme entitled *Options Women Mean Business* is run to
encourage women entrepteneurs. Like the *Cosmopolitan High Flyer*
scheme, which is also run to encourage women in business, it is
sponsored by the Trustee Savings Bank (TSB) and Nationwide
Anglia Building Society.

CONTENTS

ACKNOWLEDGMENTS

I wish to express my thanks to all my women interviewees for some fascinating and thought-provoking conversations. My apologies to the many thousands whom time – and space – prevented me from including.

My warmest gratitude to Fiona MacIntyre for her skilled and sensitive editing, and to my agent, Michael Thomas, for his support and encouragement.

Special thanks to Maggie Redman for help with the typing of this book and for providing a valuable back-up service.

INTRODUCTION

Despite the increasing numbers of women being appointed to executive or managerial-style posts, they still face fundamental problems in getting there – and staying there. These problems arise partly from men's difficulties in adjusting to the idea of female bosses, and the corresponding difficulties that women have in adjusting to a superior role.

In this book I have tried to take a positive, practical approach, pointing out some of the pitfalls likely to be encountered along the way, and recommending strategies for overcoming these. My ideas and suggestions are backed up with a wide range of case studies.

When dealing with such a vast subject as this one, it is only possible to feature a tiny number of women out of the vast pool of female talent and enterprise that thrives today in the British world of work. Those whom I have included represent a personal selection of some of the best and brightest women in business, the media and other major areas of public life. Their contributions are unique, and each has achieved success and acclaim in her own individual way, but with the shared attributes of enthusiasm, tenacity, determination and drive. I may not agree with everything they say and believe, but I defend their right to speak for themselves. In doing so they confirm what I have always suspected: that there is no single, clearcut route to the top of any career ladder, and no watertight recipe for success.

All are admirable role models for any woman wanting to make it in our highly competitive, male-dominated society. This book is a kind of survival guide for other women working their way to the top. It is also a tribute to the achievements, initiative, staying power and strength of character of some of the many remarkable women who have already got there.

Who's Who

Linda Agran
Deputy Controller of Drama, London Weekend Television.

Aged 40. Single. Her brief: commissioning and developing drama for LWT. She finds ideas and writers, works with the writer on the script, assigns producers and directors, and is involved with casting and all creative decisions throughout. Came to LWT via Warner Brothers, where she was European Head of Creative Affairs, and latterly, Euston Films, where she was one of the two chief executives.

Muriel Allen
Governor, Kingston Prison, Portsmouth.

Aged mid-fifties. Single. Joined the prison service in 1964 as an assistant governor at Holloway, where she remained for six years. From there she was posted to a girls' Borstal (now a youth custody centre). Her next move was to an open prison for women near York (as Deputy Governor), and from there to a new women's prison, Drake Hall (as Assistant Governor). She then spent two years as Senior Assistant Governor at

Durham Prison, a male prison with a thousand inmates. From Durham she moved to Prison Headquarters in London to assist with policy matters concerning women and girls in custody. And in 1982 she was appointed Governor of the male lifers' prison at Portsmouth.

Beverly Anderson
Senior Lecturer in Education, Oxford Polytechnic.

Aged 47. Separated; one son, Hamish, aged 12. Obtained BA degree in history and political science at Wellesley College, Massachusetts. Then spent four years in the Jamaica Foreign Service, after which she came to England to take a Postgraduate Certificate in Education at London University (1966–67). Married an Englishman she had met in Washington, and remained in Britain. Became a primary school teacher in East London, and, after a year, Head of Infants. Held a series of teaching posts, culminating in a headship in 1981. Has also served as a councillor with Oxford City Council, and been involved in a second career – as a broadcaster. She is perhaps best known for her work as a presenter of Channel Four's *Black on Black* series (1982–83) and BBC1's *Sixty Minutes* (1983). Is currently on the board of the Oxford Stage Company and St Martin's School of Art.

Carys Bannister
Britain's only woman neurosurgeon.

Aged early fifties. Single. Trained at Charing Cross Hospital Medical School, qualifying in 1958 with Honours in Surgery. Began her career as a House Surgeon in general surgery at Charing Cross Hospital. Became interested in neurosurgery while working at Birmingham Accident Hospital. Her first neurosurgical post was at Leeds General Infirmary where, after 18 months as Registrar, she spent nearly nine years as Senior Registrar in the Department of Neurosurgery. Since October

1975 she has worked as a Consultant Neurosurgeon at North Manchester General Hospital and Booth Hall Children's Hospital, Manchester. She is also Honorary Lecturer in Paediatric Neurosurgery at the University of Manchester School of Medicine.

Tessa Blackstone
Master, Birkbeck College, University of London, and chairperson of the BBC's General Advisory Council.

Aged 45. Divorced; one son, one daughter. Has had a distinguished and varied career as an academic, and in central and local government. Began as a part-time lecturer in sociology at Regent Street Polytechnic, London (1964–65). Her most recent appointments were with the Inner London Education Authority, first as Deputy Education Officer (Resources), then as Clerk to the Authority and Director of Education; and the Policy Studies Institute, as Rowntree Special Research Fellow (December 1986–September 1987). Received a life peerage in 1987.

Ann Burdus
Director of AGB Research PLC, the largest market research company in Europe, with a turnover of £103 million (more than half of it generated outside the UK).

Aged 54. Married; no children. Came to marketing via a degree in psychology from Durham University and worked in mental health before beginning a commercial career in market research and advertising with the international advertising agency, Ogilvy and Mather. She is a Fellow of the Institute of Practitioners in Advertising and in 1981 she chaired the Advertising Association. She is also Chairman of the EDC for Distributive Trades, a Director of Barclays Bank UK Ltd and Deputy Chairman of the Health Education Authority, with special responsibility for their AIDS campaign.

Genevieve Cooper
Deputy Editor, London Evening Standard.

Aged 41. Single. Previous journalistic experience includes: *Forum* magazine, which, in its early days, was mainly run by women; *Cosmopolitan* (in six years she moved from assistant to the Editor to Features Editor), the Mail On Sunday's *YOU* magazine (Deputy Editor) and *The Sunday Times Magazine* (as Editor).

Sally Davies
Consultant haematologist, Brent Health District.

Aged 38. Widow. Trained at Manchester University Medical School and later, the Royal Postgraduate Medical School, Hammersmith Hospital (advanced medicine course). Transferred from paediatrics into haematology. Previous posts include: Senior Registrar, Department of Haematology, Central Middlesex Hospital; Senior Registrar, North London Blood Transfusion Centre; Honorary Lecturer in Haematology, Middlesex Hospital Medical School; Honorary Senior Registrar, Bloomsbury Health Authority, London.

Maureen Foers
Hull-based entrepreneur.

Aged 48. Divorced; one daughter. The recruitment agency she started in 1971 has now grown into 'Business Resources', the largest independent, practical, commercial training centre in Britain. It provides courses, many of them funded by the MSC, ranging from teaching the office junior to type to helping the proprietor develop new ideas for business. An active committee woman, she is a member of Hull Chamber of Commerce, the Regional Training Group of the CBI, and the Humberside area's Manpower Board (to name but three).

Betty Guyatt

Currently branch manager of the Midland Bank at
Wembley Park, North London.

Aged mid-forties. Divorced; no children. Has been a manager
with the Midland for nearly 14 years, mainly in the suburbs.
Started out as an 'average clerk'. Later became a manager's
assistant at the Hounslow branch, and from there was
appointed to her first managerial role – as an assistant manager
at Twickenham in 1975. Then she moved to Kenton as
manager of the branch there ("It was a case of 'We'll give her a
little branch and see what she does with it. If she falls flat on her
face it won't cause too much damage'"). She has been very
much a role model for other women considering a career in
banking. She was an early member of Women In Banking and
is also involved in the still-embryonic Women in Midland.

Harriet Harman

MP for Peckham, one of Labour's safest London seats, since
October 1982. She is Shadow Health Minister.

Aged 37. Married (to trade union official Jack Dromey); three
children. A qualified solicitor who came to Parliament via a
non-traditional route: law centre (working with the tenants'
movement, and the trade union movement at local level), the
women's movement, and the NCCL (as legal officer she was
taking test cases under the newly formed Sex Discrimination
Act).

Betty Jackson

Fashion designer. She was awarded the MBE in autumn
1987.

Aged 38. Married, to her French partner, David; two children.
Since its launch in 1981, her company Betty Jackson Ltd., has
grown into a huge international enterprise with a turnover of

around £1.6 million, and outlets in Europe, the USA and Japan. In 1985 she was awarded the Designer of the Year trophy, a much-coveted prize in the British fashion industry. Trained at Birmingham College of Art, where she took a degree in fashion and textiles. Spent six years with Quorum as their chief designer before going it alone.

Marie Jennings
Director, Development, Public Relations Consultants Association (PRCA).

Aged 57. Married; one son, several step-children. Extensive experience in the communications industry, including: working with governments on projects ranging from the Berlin Wall to export programmes for Britain and the US; Managing Director of the first US PR consultancy to set up a London subsidiary. Former Woman of the Year (1969) and elected a Fellow of the Institute of Directors (January 1959). Current responsibilities include the following: Head of the Unit Trust Association Information Unit; Inventor and Deputy Chairman of The Money Management Council; Programme Associate on Channel 4's *Moneyspinner* TV series on personal finance; Honorary Treasurer, The National Association of Women's Clubs.

Sarah Kendall
Assistant Area Manager, Reading.

Aged 27. Single. Entered the railway industry as a graduate (read Law with French at the University of Kent). Started off at Crewe as an operations trainee ("the nuts and bolts of running trains"), working her way around each department: signalling, carriage cleaning, booking office, etc. Then went to Willesden Junction in North London, as traffic manager for 18 months – and in July 1986 to Carlisle, one of Britain's busiest InterCity stations, as Station Manager. Promoted to Reading in 1987.

Carey Labovitch
Owner and publisher of *Blitz* magazine, the *Magazine Distribution Book* aimed at newsagents (now in its fifth edition) and other titles distributed through HMV record shops.

Aged 27. Single. Started *Blitz* while a first-year student at Oxford. After leaving with a BA Hons in French and Italian, she set up the magazine professionally in Soho offices. In 1987 she was shortlisted for the Veuve Clicquot Businesswoman of the Year award, the youngest person ever to be considered for this. Other awards have included the BBC Enterprise award for small businesses (in 1985 out of 700 entries); and the Guardian's Best Graphics award.

Her company now has a turnover of £4 million and has increased its print run from the original 2,000 to 45,000.

Susi Madron
Housewife and mother with no previous business experience, she formed her own company, Cycling For Softies, in 1981.

Aged 44. Married; three children. The company specializes in a mixture of flexible pedal-powering around the French countryside and gourmet nights spent in upmarket hotels.

Vivien Padwick
Chairwoman and Managing Director, Vivair: air brokers, air travel agents and, more recently, property developers.

Aged 39. Single. The daughter of a London travel agent, she left school at 16 and chalked up a few firsts in her chequered career: the first female sales rep in the travel industry (with Godfrey Davis' car rental company); the first female sales rep for Britannia Airways, and one of the first female account executives at McCann Erickson advertising agency. In 1978, with a £1,500 loan and one (male) assistant, she launched Vivair. The company is now turning over about £20 million, her staff have grown to 24, and Vivair is Britain's number 2 air charter broker.

Jane Reed
Managing Editor, *Today* (and, until its demise in June 1987, *Sunday Today*).

Aged mid-forties. Single. Magazine background. Editor of *Woman's Own* throughout the seventies when the magazine became Britain's top-selling weekly for women. Later, became Editor-in-Chief on *Woman*, then joined the Specialist, Educational and Leisure Group of magazines in IPC as Assistant Managing Director. In December 1983, was appointed to the main board of IPC and set up the Holborn Publishing Group. Left IPC in the Autumn of 1985 to join the new national newspaper *Today*, as Managing Editor (Features).

Steve Shirley
Entrepreneur. Founder and Managing Director of *F International*, the largest independent software organization in the UK.

Aged 54. Married; one grown-up son. The company was launched in 1961, in response to Shirley's recognition of the need for working mothers to fulfil their potential and develop their careers outside the constraints of a 9–5 office environment. The company's success has earned her an OBE.

Josette Simon
One of Britain's fastest rising young actresses.

Aged 28. Single. Trained at the Central School of Speech and Drama. In 1972 joined the Royal Shakespeare Company and became one of the first black actresses to be cast in a Shakespeare play at the RSC. Many roles to her credit, including Rosaline in 'Love's Labours Lost', Martha in 'The Miracle Worker' and Maria in 'Twelfth Night'. She has also appeared in several TV plays, including the series, 'Blakes Seven'.

Linda Stoker
Managing Director of Dow Stoker Training Associates, which organizes courses for women at various levels of ability, including married women wishing to return to the workforce.

Aged 33. Married; two children. Background in PR and publicity (including the Rank organization and Guy's Health District) and training, including a position as training manager at the Tower Hotel, St Katherine's Dock, London.

Barbara Switzer
Deputy General Secretary of the manufacturing union, TASS.

Aged 47. Married; no children. Her roots are in engineering. After completing an electrical technician's apprenticeship at Metropolitan Vickers in Manchester (now GEC), she worked in detail and design draughting, with experience both in offices and on the shop floor. An apprentices' dispute aroused her interest in trade unionism. She became a union representative, going on to work at local and national level. Was elected to the union's National Executive Committee as the Deputy E.C. member for her division and then as the women's representative. In 1976 she became a full-time official, and the same year, she received the TUC Women's Gold Badge, the youngest woman ever to win it. In 1979 she was made a National Organizer with responsibilities for eleven major electrical and electronic combines, including GEC, Philips and Plessey. She is also on the Confederation of Shipbuilding and Engineering Unions' Executive.

Susan Todd
Theatre Director.

Aged 45. Single. Began her career with the Royal Shakespeare Company as Assistant to John Barton at Stratford-upon-Avon, an apprenticeship she continued via the ATV Repertory Theatre Trainee Director Scheme, working at theatres in Leicester, Derby and Canterbury. She was co-founder of the Monstrous Theatre Regiment company, and from 1980–83 worked as joint artistic director of the National Theatre of Brent. More recently, she has worked with the RSC, directing a women's project, *Heresies,* at the Pit (Barbican). Since 1980 she has also done a lot of teaching – particularly at RADA and the Guildhall School of Music and Drama.

Jean Wadlow
Managing director of Wadlow Grosvenor International, one of Britain's leading producers of corporate films and videos.

Aged 43. Divorced; no children. From secretarial college she went to a firm of London stockbrokers. She left after two years and became secretary to the Chairman of the Charles Barker advertising agency. Then began working as assistant to the agency's TV director and when he died, took over his job on a six-months trial basis. Her first assignment was a series of cinema commercials for the Midland Bank. In 1971, the company split into two separate units and she was asked to run Charles Barker Films. In 1978, she and the then chairman of Charles Barker, Kyrle Simond, bought out the company from the group. Wadlow has been the majority shareholder ever since, and her number of clients has risen from 17 to around 200. Company turnover is more than £2 million. She also runs a company specializing in teaching media presentation skills to senior managers and executives, using a purpose-built studio.

Katharine Whitehorn

Columnist with the Observer since 1960. Associate Editor, Observer, since 1980.

Aged early fifties. Married to writer Gavin Lyall; two sons. Began her journalistic career on the magazine *Home Notes* (as sub-editor of 'Real Life' love stories), then *Picture Post, Woman's Own,* the *Spectator,* and finally, the *Observer.* She also wrote the best-selling cookery book, 'Cooking in a Bedsitter', which is still in print after more than 25 years. From 1972-77 she was on the board of the British Airports Authority and is currently on the board of the Nationwide Building Society.

Carol Wilson

Former head of A and R, Polydor; one of the only female A and R chiefs – an assertive, policy-making role, unlike the more passive, servicing role of record company Press departments where women tend to dominate.

Aged mid-thirties. Single. Having studied piano and clarinet at the Royal College of Music, she began her present career as secretary to the Managing Director of Transatlantic Records, and after a couple of months went to see Richard Branson at Virgin. Branson offered her a job as head of his music publishing company, Virgin Music. She started signing up artists like the Police and Human League. From there she started her own successful label, Dindisc (in conjunction with Virgin). Later, moved to WEA Records as general manager, A and R. In November 1985 she went to Polydor.

During the writing of this book, she was sacked from Polydor after applying for (and failing to get) the managing director's job. The new managing director – a man without her track record – promptly fired her. She is now setting up her own record label – a long-cherished ambition.

1

You Know You Can Do It!

---◆---

MAKING YOUR MARK AND LOOKING THE PART

---◆---

Women are too emotional . . . too aggressive . . . too weak. They have no authority . . . are not suited to taking responsibility at work. These are just a few of the stereotypes which women have been lumbered with over the years – by men, the media and society generally. Labels which have been used as an excuse to exclude women from the corridors of power and to shackle them to low-paid, low-status jobs instead of senior managerial posts.

The O.E.D. definition of the word 'boss' is *Master* (my italics), person in authority, overseer. When we ask to see the 'manager', we often picture a sober-suited male seated behind a large desk (fat cigar an optional extra). It is hard to erase this kind of entrenched image, and we are all guilty of making such wrong assumptions in our daily lives.

Most of us, male and female, still tend to take it for granted that the person in charge of most organizations will be a man. When it turns out to be a woman, there is often an element of surprise. It happens right across the board, in most spheres of public life: industry, commerce, medicine, education, the arts and so on.

On the telephone, too, it is all too easy to assume that the female voice at the other end of the wire belongs to the boss's secretary rather than to the boss. Women in senior positions are conspicuous by their absence, so much so that such mistakes are commonplace and, to the women concerned, must be, at best, irritating, and at worst, downright insulting.

You are probably familiar with the kind of situation that arises. You telephone a number, a disembodied voice answers and connects you to an extension. A female voice speaks . . .

YOU "Can I speak to the manager/supervisor/head of department?"
SHE "This *is* the manager/supervisor/head of department."
Embarrassed pause while caller clears throat, collects wits, mumbles apologies, thinks of what to say next.

Why should this be so? Why, in the post-feminist eighties, do we see so few women at the top of their chosen profession?

Women make up 46 per cent of the work force but a mere 5.5 per cent of managers. They are, on average, six years younger than male managers and are mainly to be found in personnel and purchasing [British Institute of Management report: May 1987]. Only two per cent of company directors are women, and they account for a mere three per cent of the membership of the British Institute of Management, which has introduced courses to help women become more assertive.

Women today are still visualized in, and expected to adopt, supportive, non-assertive roles. It is all part of the way in which society is structured. Men are perceived as active, the hunters, doers, innovators; women are perceived as predominantly passive, decorative, servicers of men and children, used to putting themselves last. Such notions are still deeply rooted in our consciousness.

Girls continue to be taught from the cradle to believe that marriage and motherhood will be their ultimate source of personal fulfilment. When they grow up, they are viewed primarily in this limited fashion rather than on equal terms with men, as 'rounded' individuals capable of a wide range of achievements. "Women have been brought up ... to see themselves as supporters, aiders and abettors, sustainers, but not as bosses over other adults ... Women generally lack the experience of being the final decision-maker, someone who operates without an okay from a higher-up. Men know at a very early age that they will grow up to be responsible for themselves – they are the 'in-charge' sex. They don't long for a superior species to validate their decisions – they *are* the

— 'Intellectually, men want their wives to be better educated. Psychologically, they are unable to cope with it ... ,—

superior species and the higher authority: the chairman of the board, the president of the company, the head of the family. ..."[1]

However successful they may be in their working lives, many women become so preoccupied with the jobs and promotion prospects of their husbands or male partners that their own career needs take second place. Society expects women to forego their aspirations for the 'greater good' of the family, i.e. the career and ambitions of their male partners, their children's upbringing and development. Women's role at work becomes an extension of their role in the family, where they subordinate self-interest to the needs of others.

According to Professor Cary Cooper, Head of Organization Psychology at Manchester University, there is a paradox in the psychological battle between the sexes:

"Intellectually, men want their wives to be better educated. Psychologically, they are unable to cope with it – it's still the mother-at-home model they think about."[2]

Rosie Smith, course team chair for the Open University's 'Women into Management' course, acknowledges the very real problems of women with fragmented education and career patterns. "To ensure we have more women managers we may have to go back as far as primary school and the home to tackle sex stereotyping and parental attitudes."[3]

The differences in the way that many parents treat their sons and daughters is an important factor here. Little boys are encouraged to be enterprising, adventurous, outgoing. Their sisters are taught the virtues (sic) of dependence and submissiveness. Boys learn to take the initiative. Girls spend their time trying to please. Any deviation from these 'norms' is frowned upon.

The pressures on women to conform to 'acceptable' female images are reinforced by the media. Advertising also has a lot to answer for. It has become increasingly responsible for shaping and influencing our attitudes. Time and again, in the way it promotes a product, it plays on conventional and outmoded images of women: e.g. sex object, drudge, angel, harridan, whore, nag.

Conversely, men are depicted as self-assured, physically strong and generally dominant, within both public and private spheres.

Exceptions are so rare that it requires an effort of will to think of them. One particularly imaginative advertisement is the *Mail on Sunday* TV commercial, featuring the young man prepared to go to almost any lengths to reach his loved one, only to be spurned and rejected by her in favour of her own 'daily mail/male'.

A quick flip through the pages of the *Radio Times* and *TV Times* will reveal equally few instances of female role models in television drama. Perhaps the most obvious – and prolific – are women detective inspectors in popular police series such as BBC TV's *Juliet Bravo* series and ITV's *Cat's Eyes*.

Then there are *Cagney And Lacey* (BBC TV), who have become almost a cult duo. This series is as much about the contrasting personalities of, and dynamics between, the two women detectives as about individual storylines.

Another example is the main female character, brilliantly portrayed by Penelope Keith, in the BBC TV series, *Executive Stress*. Ms Keith plays a high-flying executive in a publishing house. Admittedly, she is working alongside her 'husband', but she has responsibility, she has *clout*. ... She is seen primarily in terms of her intellect and intelligence rather than as a dreary domestic cipher, or a butt of men's jokes. A refreshing change from the usual glut of female stereotypes in soaps and sitcoms.

How, given such few positive images to follow, can the aspiring woman executive ever begin to be taken seriously? How can she assert her authority or set about making her mark?

Shakespeare's famous saying, 'To thine own self be true', is sound advice in just about any context. It is important for a woman not to lose sight of who she really is beneath the outer image she wishes to project.

Marie Jennings, Director, Development, P.R.C.A: "I am much more impressed by someone who is *genuine*. Someone who is trying to be something they are not is pretty obvious immediately to a person who has some experience in these matters. If you are going for a job, recognize that people will judge you on what is *there* and not on what you are trying to pretend is there.

Also, I think it's important to be more realistic. ... There is no such thing as a free lunch and I think that women would benefit by recognizing that much earlier on and not trying to get something for nothing."

You may be anxious to impress your superiors, to convey an impression of stunningly cool efficiency, but if you try to alter your basic personality you could very quickly come unstuck. It is no good pretending to be what you are not. Chances are that you will not be able to keep up the pretence. Others will see through the façade and you will only end up uncomfortable inside your own skin, restless and discontented, the proverbial 'square peg'.

You will be repeating a similar pattern of behaviour to the woman who sacrifices her own ambitions for the full-time care of her family. You will be sinking your own identity, talents and aspirations in the 'corporateness' of the company.

David Gaister, who runs P.A.C.E (Performance and Communication Enterprises): "One of the challenges to women entering management today is that the role models available to them are predominantly male. ... Learning by a kind of osmosis from role models is not only time-consuming but usually means that all the behaviour displayed is copied – whether or not it is relevant or of value. ... Women can contribute far more to business by operating from their own strengths than by imitating men."[4]

Gaister advocates a non-sexist method of communicating, called neuro-linguistic programming, a 'thought process' which (he claims) helps to establish effective business skills and empathy with colleagues.

Meanwhile, as you begin your journey upwards, work out just what you think you have to offer and where your strengths and weaknesses lie. It's not a bad idea to make a list of personal 'debits' and 'credits' and work on these. Concentrate on building up a credible and arresting all-round image.

— *'Women can contribute far more to business by operating from their own strengths than by imitating men.* ,—

Success is about *power*, and there are certain basic attributes which you can cultivate in order to gain – and express – that power. They will prove vital to your prospects and do wonders for your self-esteem:

Learn to be assertive

There is a world of difference between assertiveness and aggression. To be assertive means knowing what you want and being able to express it in a firm, reasonable and non-threatening manner. That way, you will be sure to get the best out of people, both on the way up the ladder and after you hit the top rung.

Assertiveness is a skill which, like any other, can be acquired with practice. If you find this difficult, there are a number of assertiveness training courses and consciousness raising groups available (details at the end of this book). They are a valuable source of support, helping to break down the social straitjacket which is holding you back. Assertiveness is not incompatible with the more 'feminine' qualities of compassion, perceptiveness and intuition.

Compassion, perceptiveness and intuition

These are necessary and complementary assets which can be successfully deployed in the cut-and-thrust climate of the business world.

Jean Denton, former Businesswoman of the Year, says: "I hate the power games men play. I have always thought it was wrong to ask women to change themselves. That way, they become one of the boys and bring nothing new to their job."[5]

Sense of humour

Perhaps the most important asset of all, and easily the best safety valve in a crisis. Don't lose it.

Linda Agran, Deputy Controller of Drama, London Weekend TV: "I find that humour is the most important thing in my life. I cannot function without it and so, strangely enough, a lot of people think I'm quite relaxed, laid-back about my work – and jokey. In board meetings, or wherever, I'll crack a gag.

I think it's terribly important that anyone who works for me has a good time. I don't want them to think I'm authoritarian, because I'm *not*. ... I like to see smiles when I arrive. I wouldn't like people scurrying away and thinking: 'Oh Christ, she's arrived'."

Jean Wadlow, Company Director, Wadlow Grosvenor International: "Humour is essential. You couldn't work here without it."

Genevieve Cooper, Deputy Editor, London Evening Standard: "Humour is very useful in times of great stress. If you don't have a sense of humour you have a nervous breakdown! You can have both, but if you can laugh at what is happening instead of tearing your hair out and bursting into tears, which is traditionally what women are supposed to do, then it helps. Laughing could be women's biggest ally."

'If you can laugh at what is happening instead of tearing your hair out and bursting into tears, then it helps.

'

Style
First impressions are crucial, and what you wear in the office or board room can greatly affect other people's response to you and their opinions of your potential. You may feel, with some justification, that you should be judged on what you do and whether you produce the company goods rather than on whether you look the part. But, like it or not, women are still judged very much on their physical appearance.

It's a two-way thing. If you are looking good you *feel* good. You then give out more and others react to you more sympathetically.

If you want to progress within a company, try to cultivate an appropriate style from the outset. A style that strikes the right note of calm competence and authority. A style that reflects the status of a future boss. It must be suitable for your personality and suitable for the company. Aim to strike a balance between the two.

Vivien Padwick, Managing Director, Vivair: "If you are trying to get up the ladder, the first thing you do is dress the part. I've always dressed as if I was an executive, because I didn't want to be a secretary. In the first job I got as a sales rep, I spent an absolute fortune – most of my salary – on clothes.

I started selling when I was about 23, and I'm told in those days I was quite an attractive looking female. I used to do cold calling. When I went and knocked on the door at ICI, the porter would say – 'Mr Brown, I have an extremely attractive young lady to see you', and I would always get in.

> *'If you are trying to get up the ladder, the first thing you do is dress the part.'*

In those days I used to wear black clothes. I wanted to be 32 and stay there. I liked wearing anything that was sophisticated.

When I worked for *Vogue* magazine, my clothes had to be spot-on. I felt that it wasn't my job that was important but how I looked, and I didn't like that at all.

In the early days of Vivair, I remember once I had to meet two different lots of people on the same day. In the morning I had a meeting with some older, Yorkshire clients – a breakfast meeting at 8.30 at Kings Cross. At lunchtime I was going on to a holiday company. It was the days of the open-necked shirt, band round the head, the gold medallion with the hairy chest!

I completely changed my hairstyle, everything. To meet my older clients I'd worn a frumpy tweed suit with my hair up. I went back home afterwards, frizzed all my hair, put my latest gear on and thoroughly updated my appearance . . . so I suppose I do take notice about clothes and who I am going to meet.

When you are under 25 you can get away with very cheap clothes and put them together, but I think there is still a need in the market for trendy clothes for the 25-plus age group. I buy designer clothes most of the time, but the prices are extraordinarily high.

I thought at one time of opening up clothes shops to cater for myself and all my friends. We don't want that 'Establishment' look, the Alexons and Windsmoors, the 'County' type of look. It's so boring. I try to be a bit more modern than that. I like expensive, modern clothes. What I'm saying is: *Be different.*"

Carey Labovitch, owner and publisher of *Blitz* magazine: "Image is very important in the case of *Blitz* magazine. It sells all over the world and has a very strong image in the fashion/ design industry. In 1985 we organized a big event which really put *Blitz* on the map in terms of image, and obviously, I've got to live up to that all the time. We commissioned 22 international fashion designers to customize denim jackets at a fashion show in aid of the Prince's Trust (for under-privileged young people). The collection was exhibited at the Victoria and Albert Museum, then it went to the Louvre in Paris. That was wonderful.

Personally, my image is divided. Sometimes I have to be the businesswoman and dress accordingly. I might have to go to a formal lunch where I am expected to wear a business suit, and in the evening I could be going to a record company reception where I just want to be myself and wear jeans.

I try to compromise between the two. I try to develop my own style. I wear a lot of black and white. When I first started, I was more or less working for myself. I used to come to the office dressed as if I was going to college, but now I have to set a certain example even to the rest of the staff.

Just wearing the padded shoulders makes me feel better, more 'in command'."

The right kind of clothes are an excellent investment, not only financially but also when it comes to personal morale and wellbeing. Care in choosing your wardrobe will not only enhance your reputation with business colleagues, it will help *you* to gain plenty of self-confidence in the process. It will enable you to stay ahead – to be noticed.

Executive dressing is now big business as more women join the managerial ranks. There are 'image workshops', seminars on 'style', and style consultants who will come to your home and advise you on how to look your best. A woman's psychology and lifestyle are taken into account. It's expensive, but it can be money well spent if, like me, you loathe the ritual of chain-store shopping and tend to get mesmerized by the sheer volume of clothes on offer.

Hiring a style consultant cuts down the tedious process of traipsing around endless shops and changing rooms, choosing and trying on ill-fitting or unsuitable clothes, by backing up sensible advice with some ruthless ditching of ancient or rarely worn garments. In some cases the style consultant will accompany her clients on shopping expeditions. Some of the larger stores also have their own fashion consultants.

Style and flair are the watchwords. There is an art to looking good and it is far better to develop your own individual style than to be a slave to fashion. However, here are a few ground rules you can follow.

Basics

Pick clothes that are hard-wearing and of fine quality. Too many trendy, here-today-gone-tomorrow outfits might be fun but they are a false economy. Classic lines which free you to ring the changes, with different blouses and tops and varied accessories, are your best bet. Choose a smart jacket as a base for the outfits.

Accessories

A functional outfit can be transformed into an alluring one with the right accessories: the colourful scarf skilfully placed to hide a stark neckline; the unusual brooch; the attractive earrings. All these extra little touches can give added impact to your image without great expense.

Hair

Managerial women need manageable styles – nothing too elaborate, or it will start to take over your life and there aren't enough hours in the day for that *and* work. Apart from the time factor, untidy hair can ruin the effect of a stylish look.

> '*I* think the way you look is important whatever line of business you are in. They are going to react much more favourably to you if you look attractive, whether you are male or female. '

Shoes

Keep them clean, and keep abreast of changing fashions. Don't accumulate old pairs. Throw them out when they have had their day. A tatty or grubby pair of shoes makes you look anything but businesslike.

What you wear is what you are – at least in the eyes of those who meet you for the first time. Your clothes and your outward appearance are the first clue to your identity. They can be a subtle, unwritten code to the way in which you operate in the workplace.

Carol Wilson, Former Head of A and R, Polydor: "I think the way you look is important whatever line of business you are in: where you are dealing with people you don't know well – new people – they are going to react much more favourably to you if you look attractive, whether you are male or female.

I have a male friend who is very stylish and I've always used him as a great adviser on clothes. After I started working for corporations, I said to him: 'How should I dress?' and he said: 'Most of the other women you will be dealing with at work are going to be secretaries. It's important that you look different.' I'd never thought about that because I'd always felt very 'street', but I actually found that it *worked* to spend more money on expensive clothes. They are much more practical because they won't crease and fall apart.

I call it my corporate style! . . . I wear monochrome all the time – black, white, grey – and that's because I really haven't the time to think about what I'm going to wear in the morning, or ironing or anything like that. All my clothes go together because of that . . . I spend no time, ever, thinking about what to wear, except when I'm actually buying something."

Jane Reed, Managing Editor, *Today*: "As an editor you can be as flamboyant as you like, but then you go into management and have to be there at 8 a.m. because they all vie with each other to see how early they can get in. So I was worrying at first about clothes, and I decided I would do what *they* did

— '*E*verybody has to work out for themselves whether it's important to dress in a way that is appropriate to the role, or whether it's important to express themselves. , —

and have four good suits and 32 shirts and not think any more about it! That was an enormous relief.

It's very practical, classic stuff. The biggest worry is which tights to put on!"

Ann Burdus, Director of AGB Research PLC, the largest market research company in Europe: "I don't think the question of image is any different for men or for women. I think everybody has to work out for themselves whether it's important to dress in a way that is appropriate to the role, or whether it's important to express themselves. If they decide on the latter, they mustn't be surprised if they are then penalized in the work role. . . .

Certainly, I think girls who are *provocative* in their dress shouldn't be surprised if they are not taken particularly seriously. Men who expect to be taken seriously, dress the part, and I think women have to as well.

I have always dressed in an extremely conservative way. I wear business suits and blouses, I have matching handbags and shoes, and have done for the last twenty years. And why not?"

The style you choose will depend not only on your size, shape and personality, but also on the kind of organization in which you work. The more conventional areas of employment, such as banking, law, accountancy and insurance, will generally demand more formal wear: the elegant, well-fitting dress, or classic shirt-blouse with trousers or skirt. Avoid too many floppy bows and mannish suits unless they are the styles that suit you best, as they are fast becoming 'clone-wear' for executive women.

Betty Guyatt, bank manager, North London (a branch of the Midland Bank): "I try not to ape men. I don't like too many suits and so on. It might look frightfully smart, but I don't want to be thought of as a man. If you look at most men, they look like clones of each other: the haircuts are the same, the glasses. . . .

I like to look well dressed. Cut and quality are important. I think it's about credibility and authority. A neat and tidy appearance breeds confidence, doesn't it?"

On the other hand, if you work in the media (advertising, P.R., the film industry), where the mood is more laid-back, you can afford to be more adventurous. Female colleagues are likely to be keener, more flamboyant followers of fashion than in more conservative professions – an extra source of competition which could prove stimulating! You can experiment with more outrageous *colours*, too.

You will quickly be able to gauge how far you can go without losing that essential air of authority which will carry you on and up the executive ladder.

> *'I think that education and confidence are what women need most to be successful.'*

So, always look presentable. Remember: first impressions count a great deal, not only with clients with whom you may be dealing but also colleagues and subordinates whom you meet on a day-to-day basis.

It's never too early to start setting an example, both in the way you behave and the way you dress. You, too, can become a role model!

Linda Agran, Deputy Controller of Drama, London Weekend TV: "There are certain things in one's life that one never forgets. I was invited to go and address the Cambridge Industrial Society at the University a few years ago. I asked them why they had asked me and one of them said: 'Because you're a role model'. It was just about the most thrilling thing that I've ever had said to me. I was really moved by it." (She was one of the two top executives at Euston Films at the time).

Beverly Anderson, Senior Lecturer in Education, Oxford Polytechnic: "I think that education and confidence are what women need most to be successful. My personal life hasn't been very successful so far, but my professional life has been, and I have been able to *survive* in that I earn my own living and have a certain amount of control over what I do in my working life because of my education and capacity for work.

I was a fairly clever child, the eldest of four whose parents gave us all (three girls and a boy, the youngest) an equal education. My father was a prosperous businessman and I went to a series of boarding schools in Jamaica from the age of five and stayed there until I was 18, along with my sisters. The section of Jamaica I come from was a very privileged one, and all my friends had the same sort of upbringing.

My father was certain that the way to survive was to be independent, and the way to be independent was to have a profession. He was very keen on my being a doctor, my headmistress was keen on my being a lawyer, and in Jamaican terms those were perfectly reasonable things to urge a girl to do.

So I was highly educated, and because of that, I think, I had a freedom which many women don't seem to have. Sometimes it seems to me that women get trapped into accepting humiliating situations because they need the money and have no other choice. What my parents bought for me, through my education, was choice. I grew up with the idea that I would support myself and that I was capable of doing anything I wanted, and that has been my attitude all along.

Although my father was born in 1898 and was a pretty standard Edwardian, he was a fair-minded man.

At home we had a traditional arrangement where my mother was supported by my father and encouraged us to regard him as Lord of the Harem. On the other hand, he always taught us to be energetic, independent, proud of ourselves and ambitious."

A watershed in her life was her experience of university in America. She read history and political science at Wellesley College, one of the Ivy League girls' colleges, and it had a profound effect on her.

"What Wellesley did for me was not only to enhance my

confidence but teach me a certain brisk egalitarianism. I have a lot of American cousins and the whole American attitude is that you call a spade a spade. You are encouraged to say: 'I'm good at certain things and not good at certain other things'. That's not boasting, it's just being businesslike – and that sort of outlook reinforced my own businesslike upbringing, which was to encourage hard work, independence and a sense of honour.

One irksome aspect of British culture, compared with American culture, is that it is regarded as important here to pretend that success is an accident. You are encouraged to *deny* confidence, because to assert it is to boast, so you pretend that it is all effortless.

This strikes me as false modesty. The problem for women in this sort of society is that it is much more difficult for them to learn how to be successful. I don't understand why I can't honestly say: 'This is what I'm good at', without people thinking: 'Isn't she brash, vulgar or whatever'."

— '*D*on't make any short cuts. Do everything thoroughly. And do it your own way.* ,* —

Carey Labovitch, owner and publisher of *Blitz* magazine: "I came across a lot of problems when I began publishing *Blitz*, basically because I'm a girl but also because I'm a *young* girl and therefore everybody knew I was inexperienced and a Bright Young Thing straight out of college. The distribution side of publishing is completely male-oriented. Women are only in the more junior positions. I know no other woman who started in that way or without a lot of experience behind her.

Many people wouldn't take me seriously at first: anything from printers trying to get a piece of the action in order to give me a reduction in price, to other publishers trying to get in there first.

I'm quite a shy, nervous person but, on the other hand, very ambitious. I just had to kick myself and say: 'Right, this is what I want out of life and I'm going to get it, whatever it costs'.

You just have to teach yourself to be very hard. It's never been a question of my being a woman as opposed to a man. I'm not a feminist. I just want people to realize that I can do as good a job as anyone else – and I've proved it. We've won three major awards since 1983.

One thing that has helped is that, as we are the youngest publisher in the country we have attracted a lot of Press over the years.

It is quite upsetting that there are so few women in this business. I have had to fight my way up, and it's only now, after more than six years, after producing this (Magazine Distribution) book which is like the Bible of the trade, that I can walk in and people know who I am without thinking: 'Oh, right little upstart.'

It's a question of getting up and motivating yourself. There is no distinct talent involved, just pure motivation and hard work. Sacrifice? – social, financial and sleep!"

Jean Wadlow, company director, Wadlow Grosvenor International: "I think the best bit of advice I can give any woman is to enjoy being a woman. . . .

Don't make any short cuts. Do everything thoroughly. And do it your own way. If you try to do it a man's way it's unnatural. I mean, the way I run this company wouldn't be the same as the way a man runs it. It wouldn't be the same style. What is *my* style? High-quality professionalism, the best in the market."

2

Moving Up

STRATEGIES FOR ADVANCEMENT

Traditionally, most working women have been used to playing second fiddle, to taking orders rather than giving them. It can be hard to adjust to a dominant, competitive role – to taking the lead. Instead of thinking in terms of a definite career plan, most women have been taught to regard work as a temporary break between school or university, and 'settling down' (i.e. marriage and motherhood).

Alternatively, if we resume paid work after our children have reached their teens, our earnings are often seen merely as an optional extra to be set aside for family holidays or other treats.

Our society is geared to the aims, aspirations and interests of the male breadwinner. Women's needs in the workplace are generally ignored. Organizations and institutions are run by men, for men, and women are expected to fit in. There is little sign of space or leeway being made to accommodate women into these masculine strongholds.

Maternity leave is a relative innovation, a token gesture to women's equality at work. It exists in theory, though under certain specific conditions, and in practice, it can be difficult for a woman to be absolutely sure that her temporary absence from the workplace has not jeopardized her promotion chances.

In order to qualify for the statutory 29 weeks' leave after the birth of her child, and the right to resume her career at the same level, a woman must have been employed by a company for at least two years before the beginning of the eleventh week of her expected confinement. She must also have worked for a minimum of 16 hours per week.

The same entitlements apply if she has been employed by the same company for at least five years and for between eight and sixteen hours a week.

But, according to the Equal Opportunities Unit, only about fifty per cent of pregnant women have the right to return to their previous jobs, either because they do not fulfil the above conditions, or because the firms which employ them are too small (firms employing less than six people are exempt from the official ruling on the employment rights of expectant mothers and can in theory refuse to reinstate a woman who stops work to have a baby).

Despite the fact that more than 65 per cent of mothers of young children now go out to work, child care facilities based in the workplace are virtually non-existent in Britain – except in the larger consortia like some national newspapers or the BBC.

Some companies, recognizing the economic waste and futility of losing high-flying women to child care are taking a more enlightened approach to the question of working mothers. Other, more flexible, options being explored include 'career break' schemes. Banks have been in the forefront here. Several years ago, the National Westminster Bank introduced a re-entry scheme, allowing staff with senior management potential to take a break of up to five years in order to look after their children. Participants are expected to work for a minimum of two weeks during each year of absence, with the guaranteed offer of re-employment at the same level as when they left.

Other banks have since followed suit, developing similar ideas. The Midland Bank's scheme is open to both women and men from senior secretarial staff upwards, while Barclays Bank allow eligible employees to take two career breaks of two years each.

> *'Once you have been sitting behind a typewriter, that is how you are perceived and it's difficult to get away from that.'*

Any measures that can help to ease the work/home dilemma faced by so many women, are to be applauded, but the incidence of such help is rare. The low priority given to working mothers makes us the poor relation of most of our European neighbours. According to the Manpower Services Commission, Britain makes the least provision for under-fives' day care of any country in Europe. Angela Phillips, arguing in favour of a more integrated social policy for child care in Britain, cites a study of 186 contemporary non-industrial societies. In only five of these were children found to be almost exclusively cared for by their mothers. Much of the rest of the non-English-speaking world, she points out, spreads the responsibility for child care away from individual families.

"In France the regular ante-natal chat for pregnant mothers does not focus on breast-feeding but on providing a rundown of all the vast array of child-care facilities and benefits available. . . ."[6]

And in the United States, San Francisco has a law requiring developers of major new commercial office space to provide rent-free accommodation, or money in lieu, for child care.

British women are expected to make their own child care arrangements, and they are not exactly spoiled for choice. State provision of child care has decreased in recent years due to draconian government cuts in nursery places. According to one recent survey, only nine per cent of under-fives whose mothers work full time are in day nurseries. A further 23 per cent are cared for by childminders.[7] Most crèches and nurseries are vastly over-subscribed, and finding the right nanny or childminder can be something of a lottery. The difficulties this poses merely serve to reinforce the sense of guilt experienced by many working women about going out to work and 'neglecting' their children – the Bad Mother syndrome.

Small wonder that, with such fundamental obstacles in their way, so many women are discouraged from actively pursuing their careers. The sheer logistics of the 'home versus work' equation are daunting (see chapter 5).

However, as our numerous case studies show, it *can* be done, given the right amount of determination, persistence and stamina. Back-up from partners can be a vital factor, too.

You may be undecided at first as to precisely what your goals are and what you wish to achieve. Sometimes, it is easier to recognize what you *don't* want. You may know that you are ambitious and capable of much more than a tedious typing job, but you may need clear guidance on which direction to take.

If your firm lacks a formal career structure, where do you begin? If you want to succeed in your own right within your chosen field, then avoid getting stuck in the secretarial trap because, in the majority of cases, trap it most certainly is. While shorthand and typing are admirable skills in their way, treat them as useful appendages, nothing more. They are a means to an end, not an end in itself. Something to fall back on, as mothers (mine included) usually say in their defence.

However high your speeds, accurate your transcripts or charmingly efficient your telephone manner, it is a myth to believe that the secretarial path will eventually lead to promotion and executive status. More often than not, it turns out to be a cul-de-sac and the competent secretary can quickly change into the frustrated office manager. Her boss will rue the day she leaves, disgruntled and undervalued, for better things. She will have become much too good to promote.

True, there will always be the shining exception to the golden rule, the woman who – through a combination of luck, talent, good judgement and sheer tenacity – beavers her way up through the ranks to grab the boss's chair and company car, the woman whose speeds and smile act as a springboard to success, an asset and not a handicap, the woman who just happens to be in the right place at the right time for her particular skills and ambitions to be recognized.

A woman like **Linda Agran**, Deputy Controller of Drama, London Weekend TV, for example: "I had no qualifications whatever. I came up the secretarial route. My first job was in the travel office of the Dunlop Rubber Company, and from there I got a job with a theatrical agent. That was my first taste of this business.

My major break came when I became European Head of Creative Affairs for Warner Brothers. I was about 25 and from there I was lured away to Euston Films where I stayed for 10½ years.

Verity Lambert and I have had very similar careers. The difference between us is that Verity got a job at the BBC and was a *dreadful* secretary and I was an extremely good one – which was a big mistake. I used to love anticipating my boss's every wish and, if I heard him on the phone saying he was going to meet someone in Geneva, I'd be on the other line booking tickets!

So, when I started to make noises about wanting more responsibility, I just got another five pounds a week and was told to read the scripts at the same time if I wanted to.

As I try to tell women now – once you have been sitting behind a typewriter, that is how you are perceived and it's difficult to get away from that. . . . The moment you start to have a man's position, in the minds of many men you devalue their jobs."

A 1983 survey by Rosalie Silverstone and Rosemary

Towler, of the City University Business School, revealed that today's female executives are more likely to be graduates and to begin their working lives as management trainees rather than secretaries. Sixty per cent of secretaries questioned considered they had no promotion prospects, and four out of five felt that they were in dead-end jobs with no future.[8]

Since that survey, the coming of the word processor has made the secretary's lot even more soul-destroying in some ways. A group of feminist secretaries calling themselves *Typecaste* object to the low social status given to secretaries, and the proprietorial attitude of many bosses towards them. Male bosses, they feel, regard secretaries as members of a different species, some kind of private arrangement on the side, making it extremely difficult for them to move on.[9]

SOGAT General Secretary, Brenda Dean, addressing a 1986 conference at which the first awards for positive action for girls in education and training were made, said: "My perception of myself . . . was to be a highly qualified female

> *I used to say that I was lucky. Now I look back and I don't think it was anything to do with luck. It is just hard work – and absolute enthusiasm.*

secretary to a male boss. I would probably get married and have a couple of children and go back to work for pin money.

People say to me: 'How did you get to do what you are doing?' I'm always interested to see their faces when I say it was pure fluke. No career was planned for me – I almost stumbled into it. Doors opened and I walked through them."

Many of my interviewees repeated this version of events,

making their rise to fame sound almost an accident of fate, rather than the result of careful forethought. A typical case of women underestimating themselves, perhaps?

Luck may be one factor, but there is certainly more to it than that, more to being successful than being in the right place at the right time. ***Vivien Padwick***, Managing Director of Vivair: "I used to say that I was lucky. Now I look back and I don't think it was anything to do with luck. It is just hard work – and absolute enthusiasm."

All my interviewees share a basic *drive* in their makeup which propelled them onwards and upwards.

Marie Jennings, Director of Development, P.R.C.A.: "I never had a clear idea of where I wanted to end up, but I have an insatiable curiosity. If I see an open door I will walk through it. It's as simple as that. I also have a great personal need to innovate."

Interestingly enough, research carried out in America in 1982 showed that the composite senior woman executive had no career goal when she started working. The survey listed various attributes needed for success, including desire for responsibility, positive attitude and persistence, all of which are strongly evident in the case studies I have selected for this book.

Marie Jennings was brought up in India during the war and went to school in Kashmir. "During all the problems of the Partition, my parents – to keep my mind off the very real physical dangers – had me taught shorthand and typing in Delhi during the riots. I've got a lovely certificate saying I was 'a nice young lady of clean habits'!

After the war I came back to Britain and there was no possibility then of going to university, so I started working for a living as a secretary for an oil company. That was where I began to hone up on my writing interests.

Then I was headhunted by an American PR company and learned the business by setting up a minuscule London office for them. (They had offices in Frankfurt, Milan and other places). I was with them for 13-odd years.

I made the break from being a secretary in the way that a lot of girls still do, because if you are standing behind the boss's desk ... people will recognize the ones who have 'edge' and give them chances to do things.

I learned a lesson from a (late) friend of mine, Jules Thorne, an entrepreneur, that the young person who succeeds is possibly not the person who tells the boss what to do all the time but who does their own job ten per cent better than normal.

Public relations is an area where day-to-day business skills are recognized as more and more important. I tell young women – men, too – that if you want to get into this business, for God's sake learn your shorthand and typing. It means that you are more immediately attractive. Shorthand is always useful. I use mine every day of the week.

I will never ever hire anyone in any capacity who can't work for themselves – like type a letter, handle a meeting. . . ."

> *'The young person who succeeds is possibly not the person who tells the boss what to do all the time but the person who does their own job ten per cent better than normal.'*

Jean Wadlow is another woman who crossed the great divide from secretary to executive. "I pushed – just pushed."

She would never ask anyone to do anything that she is not prepared to do herself. "When a colleague and I started this company we used to run up and down Wardour Street delivering films as runners. . . . I would still do it if necessary."

Linda Agran says she is as good a typist as anyone who has ever worked for her and would never ask a secretary to do something she herself would not do.

It's an irony that despite her undervalued status, very often it is the secretary who acts in a quasi-managerial role, running the office in her boss's absence, an indispensable surrogate. In his presence she is frequently a powerful intermediary between

> '*Always try and reach for the top, even if you know you'll never get there. If you get halfway there, you'll have done brilliantly.*'

boss and client, keeping unwanted callers at bay, knowing as much about the company and how it operates as her boss does.

But she rarely gets the credit or kudos that is her due, and it is only after she has flown to better prospects that the boss's frustration sets in. Absence makes the boss grow fonder. . . .

Vivien Padwick, Managing Director of Vivair, believes that all of us, men and women alike, underestimate ourselves. "When I was about 21 a boyfriend said to me: 'Always try and reach for the top, even if you know you'll never get there. If you get halfway there, you'll have done brilliantly'. I think that applies to females more than males. The average little girl at school thinks: 'Someday I'll get married and before then I'll have a super job' . . . and I wonder whether a lot of girls today, however career-minded, are not still treating that job only as a stopgap?"

Vivien believes women are subject to a second negative trait: "Even when women are slowly climbing up the ladder they

will still turn round and befriend the secretary or typist instead
of socializing with their peers – i.e. the men.

The men don't think much of you if you do that. They see it
almost as a betrayal. One gang is the executives, another is the
typists. A lot of women can giggle in the cloakroom and talk
about hairstyles. When I worked for other companies prior to
Vivair, I tended to align myself with my male colleagues.

I don't mean to be nasty or derogatory and ignore the
females, no way, but it's like the difference between a third
former and a sixth former.

Obviously, there are exceptions. If you have a friend that is
still only a typist, that's different."

You have to be extremely astute in order to predict your
chances of discarding the secretarial tag in favour of a more
personally fulfilling option. The transition is not an easy one. Is
it worth staying on, in the hope that your true worth will some
day be recognized? Or should you take a calculated risk and
seek out newer, more fruitful pastures? Should you opt for the
familiar – or the unknown?

If you are a management trainee, you will also need to look
to the future and weigh up your chances. In either case, your
decision will depend not only on job availability but on your
temperament. How patient are you? How much staying
power do you have? Are you prepared to play the waiting
game in the short-term for the sake of possible long-term
gains?

If you are reasonably contented in your present organization
and feel there are genuine prospects for advancement, then
hang on in there. This is Option Number One.

However, if you feel you are languishing in a backwater
where your special qualities and talents are being stifled, try
Option Number Two: cut your losses and look elsewhere.

In the days before the Sex Discrimination Act of 1975,
Vivien Padwick used to apply for jobs that specified male
applicants, signing her name 'V.F. Padwick'. "I'd get to the
interview, answer all their questions correctly, and when they
said: 'You're exactly right for the job, but we don't want a

female', I then had a reason to say to them: 'Well, why not?' They said: 'You'll get married' ... 'Well, I haven't got a boyfriend at the moment', I'd say, and 'I've no intention of getting married'.

Then they'd ask if I wanted children – and so on. .... At least it gave me the opportunity to confront the issues – and I always got the job. It was on a trial basis and at half the salary a man would have got, but it was those *tries* that gave me a chance.

I left my biggest company, Britannia Airways, because they said there was nowhere for me to go. I was doing more business than all the men put together, but they all got promoted and I didn't. It really is a very male-oriented world."

If you decide to move on, arm yourself with a comprehensive CV and at least two glowing references. Some firms specialize in compiling customized CVs and if time is of the essence, then it might be worth finding out about these. They advertise regularly in the 'quality' Press.

Remember that nowadays competition is likely to be fiercer than it's ever been. In the flower power era of the Sixties, there was plenty of work to be had and job-hopping became the accepted norm. Young people were in a position to pick and choose from the vast array of jobs on offer, although most women were worse off in terms of job status and pay. The women's movement had yet to make an impact and the fight for equal rights had scarcely begun.

Today's shrinking jobs market calls for a much tougher, more disciplined approach to the whole concept of work. With unemployment in Britain today nudging four million, we do not have the luxury of unlimited choice. To a certain extent, women are victims of the recession. Although we now have the Equal Pay Act and the Sex Discrimination Act, there is the attitude in some quarters that we are 'stealing men's jobs' and that men, as traditional breadwinners, should get first bite of the 'situations vacant'.

Do not let this kind of reactionary rubbish hold you back. Women have been expected to take a back seat for too long already. So – think positively. Act positively – and professionally. Don't be deterred by one or two rejections. Believe in yourself and your ability to bounce back.

You could look at it this way: the limited choice of jobs helps to concentrate our minds more effectively, channelling our energies into making earlier decisions about career goals.

In doing so we should be prepared to compromise in order to reap the benefits later on. We must not expect too much too soon.

'I don't think there is a quick way to the top. The way to the top is taking things logically, one step at a time.'

Marie Jennings, Director, Development, P.R.C.A.: "I don't think there is a quick way to the top. The way to the top is taking things logically, one step at a time. That makes for a stable development rather than a situation where you might rise to a dizzy height in two years and fall flat on your face during the third year."

Another factor you should consider when balancing your options – to stay or to leave – is whether you want to be a big fish in a small pool or a smaller fish in a larger, deeper pool where the risk of sharks is greater but the ladder is higher and there is more of a career structure. The smaller pool might have fewer rungs to negotiate, but competition may be more intense. It could be a family-type firm ruled over by a dynasty of diehards who are suspicious of bright young newcomers, especially if they happen to be female. You will be more conspicuous, more on show, and one wrong or silly move will immediately expose you to the critical gaze of your colleagues.

Taking Option One: having decided to stay put, sound out your boss or the head of department about your prospects for promotion within the company. 'If you don't ask you don't get', as the popular saying goes. Make your position clear: that much as you like the company, you are not content to stay there forever and vegetate. You feel you are capable of more responsibility and would welcome a chance to broaden your working horizons, on a trial basis if necessary, though not at the expense of pay and conditions.

Linda Agran, Deputy Controller of Drama, London Weekend TV: "I've always said to women that in a way you should create your own job. Find something that somebody needs doing, take it over and do it. Before you know where you are, you will actually be head of whatever that happens to be.

Make it clear from the outset that you have no intention of spending the rest of your days making coffee and taking memos.

And don't ever sleep with a man and believe it's going to give you any chance at all, because they are worse gossips than women are and all it will get you is a reputation."

Unlike Vivien Padwick, she believes in finding a female ally within the company. "Don't alienate women. . . . Very often younger, fluffier models are taken on board and they are so busy befriending the male executives or the boss that they forget about women.

I think it is going to be more and more important – as progress is made, and as we start to get power – that women are united."

If you have a good rapport with your boss, she or he may not need much prompting to point you in the right direction. You may be recommended for promotion or, in the meantime, assigned some of the more intellectually flexing tasks.

Vivien Padwick, Managing Director, Vivair: "One problem in getting promoted internally is that if you are too good at your current job people don't want to lose you. You've usually got a team of men against you – probably a boss who is *for* you, but most men are pretty weak and don't want to upset the apple cart. I've been in a position where I've got on extremely well with the chairman, managing director and my boss, but they've all been scared about what the other directors and sales reps would say.

> *'Don't ever sleep with a man and believe it's going to give you any chance at all, because they are worse gossips than women . . .'*

I have girlfriends who, when a vacancy came up, have been asked by their boss: 'Should we promote *Mr* So-and-so?' One friend of mine said to her boss that *she* was hoping for the promotion. The boss was astounded because she was a female and had always been there and was very good at her job.

She got the promotion but on a trial period only and at a much reduced salary, but was given the opportunity and has held the job."

When an ex-boss of hers was made redundant, **Linda Stoker** stepped into his shoes – but again, the terms were different. Her salary was about £40.00 a week less than her predecessor's, her title was altered from Controller of Publicity to Publicity Officer and the previous incumbent's company car did not appear and was never mentioned again.

If your boss is a woman, she may be particularly reluctant to delegate. To a certain extent, this is understandable. To get where she is, the woman executive has probably had to fight twice as hard as her male counterpart. By the same token, she may feel similarly driven once she has got there. She may feel compelled to go on proving herself. In our dog-eat-dog society you will always find people who are resentful of your success, just waiting for an opportunity to topple you from your rightfully earned perch. Professional jealousy is a sad fact of life.

I once worked in a publishing house for a woman editor who was a real workaholic. She was forever whingeing about her workload, and yet refused to delegate anything except the most menial tasks. Hers was a classic case of the Queen Bee syndrome: the wish to identify and collude with other *men* in the belief that any woman can make it and any woman who fails to make it only has herself to blame.

Behind her mounting heap of manuscripts, she smoked incessantly and aged rapidly. Because of pressure of work she frequently left the office early nursing a migraine while I, grossly *under*worked, quietly fumed and emptied her evil-smelling ashtrays.

After six months I quit. The consent – and relief – were mutual. I moved to another publisher's as assistant copywriter in their overseas sales department. My boss, a woman, gave in her notice that same week (it was nothing personal: she had a better offer elsewhere), the company decided not to replace her and so I achieved instant promotion: a job with interest, status – and my own secretary. I was a boss!

Women in authority may see other women lower down the ladder as potential usurpers. It is important to try to learn from this and not repeat the pattern when *you* find yourself treading the corridors of power.

Few of the women I spoke to, however, showed any Queen Bee tendencies. In fact, many went out of their way to stress their commitment to encouraging other women along the right career track.

Jane Reed, Managing Editor, *Today*: "I do this all the time. To be honest, I haven't come across those women who are supposed to keep people below them off the ladder. Most women I know have always encouraged other women, because you know your own gender very well and you can look at somebody and say: 'She's as good as him, but if she's brought up two kids I know that she's got that extra quality of X that I'm looking for.' . . ."

Katharine Whitehorn, Journalist: "A lot of us around try desperately to nurture the younger women coming up. I always take the newcomer girl out to lunch. . . .

I believe very strongly in women looking after the prospects of younger women, and if they don't (or can't), it's a measure of their own insecurity."

Carol Wilson, Former Head of A and R, Polydor Records: "I look at women and I see their potential, whereas a lot of men can't seem to recognize potential in women. I think it's all to do with role models. Women never come to me for a job in A and R and I feel it's because they look at A and R men and think: 'They're all men. I can't identify with that', and male bosses, when they're looking for A and R people, think: 'Well, the sort of person we want is a *guy* who does *this*' . . . you know. I think because of the way women are brought up, they pay more

> *I believe very strongly in women looking after the prospects of younger women, and if they don't it's a measure of their own insecurity.*

attention to detail, they are more conscientious . . . and I've always found the major difference between men and women is that men are brought up to think of their short-term ambitions whereas women are brought up to think of the good of the *whole*. Women put the company before themselves.

Linda Agran, Deputy Controller of Drama, London Weekend TV: "Women are more committed *because* of the difficulties they've had. I mean, I'd like to run up against women who are *not* good at their jobs. I really would like to meet some of the women executives who are as hopeless as some of the men. . . .

I actively encourage women. I would rather employ women than men. I find them much more supportive. I get on much better with women than men.

I remember one American woman writer who said that she could survive without a man in her life but if you really want to kill her, take away her women friends. And that's exactly the way I am. I like to be around women, to work with women. I think they are much less Machiavellian. We don't get involved

— '*Men get away with murder, in my view, but then I think we've only got ourselves to blame because so many women do let people down . . .* ' —

in the power struggle because we tend to be excluded from it. We just keep our heads down and get on with the work."

She claims to have encountered no resentment from women lower down the ladder. "I've always told every woman who's worked for me to go for my job. They ain't gonna get it, but if they are really good I'll make them a producer, I'll move them somewhere. . . .

A lot of women hold women back, because they know there are so few women who are going to get on in the company. It's like Catch 22. They sit there and think: 'Who are *you* to come in here? You've only been here five years and I've been here twenty. . . .' That is because they know there will only be, within any organization, a tiny percentage of women who will make it.

So men have their allies in those sorts of women, because the job is done *for* them."

Jean Wadlow, Managing Director of Wadlow Grosvenor International, thinks men and women have different attitudes and motivations. "What used to bore me when I worked at the advertising agency, was these regular management meetings. Instead of thinking of how to get more clients and more business, the men would always be talking about their cars and getting a space in the garage. Men are motivated by those sorts of things, and women are not.

Men get away with murder, in my view, but then I think we've only got ourselves to blame because so many women do let people down . . . I had a marvellous secretary for about five years. Excellent. Knew me, knew how I liked things done, beautiful typist, everything, and I suddenly felt 'This is not fair on her' and I promoted her to be an assistant producer (in my Audio Visual Department).

It was a total disaster. She couldn't cope. She had all the encouragement that anybody could have given her. She was my protégé. It didn't work out . . ."

Hilary Sears, an executive search consultant with Carré Orban, agrees that women can be their own worst enemies. Women not only tend to be more 'risk-averse' than men, but "there is still that lingering attitude of 'I made it by myself, so *she* ought to, too'. This is very disheartening and not at all supportive.

We women also tend to hang back. We don't push enough for recognition, money and the same benefits as men get."

Tessa Blackstone, Master, Birkbeck College: "When I was an undergraduate it never occurred to me that I had the kind of academic ability to become a university teacher and researcher. I happened to be very lucky. I was in the social sciences at a time when they were expanding and there were large numbers of recruits being taken on by the universities in the mid to late sixties. Had I been born ten years earlier, I would probably not have got an academic job, and ten years later, likewise, so in a sense I was on a kind of escalator and just kept on up it.

In some ways I think that deep down inside I'm not a scholar and therefore not suited to be a conventional, straight academic but wanted to involve myself in public life and public policy-making in a more general sense.

I haven't worked as an academic all my career and have moved around much more than most academics in the UK tend to do. I went into central government through being a member of the Central Policy Review Staff, then back into the academic world, then into local government as a local authority chief officer.

On the whole I don't feel I've been discriminated against. In some senses I feel I have been fortunate in that I have been pursuing a professional career at a time when more and more organizations feel under pressure to recruit senior women."

If you are new to the company you will have to win the trust and acceptance of older male colleagues who may have been there for a lot longer. This could be a slow and painful process calling for much diplomacy, as **Sarah Kendall** discovered when she first joined the railway industry.

After her year's training she accepted an appointment as traffic manager at Willesden Junction, an unpopular base.

"I felt I would rather get stuck into a tough job than an easier option, so that I could say afterwards: 'Look, I have done that!' It was acknowledged that it was a tough job for anyone, carrying a certain amount of status. There was the attitude: 'She must be hard as nails'.

Earning the respect of my colleagues was the hardest part. I had a lot of problems at first – hostility . . . Not so much 'We are going to give you a hard time' (nobody deliberately did you down) but 'You are on your own. We are not going to help you.'

In the initial training year, it was quite an easy situation to go and watch someone else doing a job, but when you are forced to make decisions you really are the boss. I was thrown in and expected to cope. There is quite a gap between the kind of things covered in the training and what you were expected to face up to later on. Nobody tells you what to do at three in the morning when one of your booking offices is on fire (at Bushey Station). You have on-call responsibility. . . .

Another time, one of my stations was left open all night. The police were called in. There was no sign of any staff, and a trail of blood down the corridor. I got a call: 'Please come and

> *If you are new to the company you will have to win the trust and acceptance of older male colleagues who may have been there for a lot longer.*

see what's going on'. The training hadn't prepared me for this sort of thing. You need grim determination, the skin of a rhinoceros, a deaf ear and a blind eye."

Throughout the British Rail network only six out of 16,000 drivers are women and there are under a hundred female guards, yet women make up 12,000 of the railways' workforce of 140,000.

In 1987 B.R. launched a campaign to recruit more women drivers and also hopes to attract more female guards and signal staff. This is in response to the 1986 EOC (Equal Opportunities Commission) report attacking B.R. for discriminating against women employees.

Since the report, fifty per cent of staff hired for white-collar jobs have been female, the highest ever proportion.

In the early stages of your journey up the corporate ladder, learn as much about the organization – its history, aims, policy – as you can. Do your homework. Get to know the firm inside out, engage in its daily happenings (however mundane) and delight in its achievements so that you are completely au fait with how it functions.

It's not a bad idea to get into the habit of presenting your boss with a typewritten list of suggestions for heightening departmental efficiency – for example, ideas for cost-cutting or improving feedback.

Take the initiative. Grasp the nettle. Don't wait to be *asked* to do something. Show your enthusiasm – and commitment – by *doing*. Remember: nothing worthwhile in this world was ever achieved without some measure of risk attached. Nothing ventured, nothing gained. Playing safe may shield you from mistakes, but it won't get you far in the hurly-burly of life. So, if you spot an opportunity, go for it, even if the end result might fall short of perfection. Forget the Superwoman syndrome, the need to please everyone all the time. It is unrealistic and will only give you ulcers (see chapters 5 and 6).

Being assertive means being willing to take the occasional gamble – and not losing sleep over it (or your sense of humour). It means accepting the possibility of error. It means

> '*Learn to accept criticism and do not interpret it as a personal attack on your virtue.*'

taking responsibility for one's actions. It does *not* mean riding roughshod over the feelings and ideas of your colleagues or subordinates, taking their loyalty for granted, or throwing your weight around the office.

Always listen. Listening is not a passive activity. On the contrary: it teaches you to be patient and stops you from being too impulsive or arrogant. Listening to the *tone* of someone's voice as well as to the actual words helps you to understand the other person's inner feelings and motivation (as well as what is actually being said).

So many people only half-listen, and it is then that many wrong messages get transmitted, misunderstandings occur and mistakes are made. So listen and absorb, and if you still don't fully understand the meaning of the message don't be afraid to ask.

Learn to accept criticism and do not interpret it as a personal attack on your virtue. Look on it as grist to your managerial mill and skills. Store it up in your mind for future reference so that when *you* are the boss you will be better equipped to deal with the peccadilloes of your own team. Being able to take criticism without rancour means being prepared to learn from our mistakes and to admit our fallibility as human beings. It means being receptive to the observations of others. It means a flexible, adaptable outlook – vital attributes in the minefield of business.

If your boss is locked into the Neanderthal mould and assumes you will spend the rest of your working life happily servicing his needs, then don't waste time hoping he will change tack. That type of man rarely does. Get out while you are still on speaking terms. Avoid any mud slinging, because mud sticks and you can't afford to pass up a decent reference.

When you do decide to leave, don't burn your boats. However miffed you may be feeling, make sure you have another job lined up first. Mysterious gaps in your CV will only provoke unwanted questions from prospective employers.

If you need career advice from someone with no axe to grind, then a session with a vocational guidance expert might prove beneficial. According to Joshua Fox, a consultant psychologist with Career Analysts, men are conditioned to think 'I must' and women to think 'I can't'. "Our job is to break through that kind of conditioning and try to match people as *individuals*."

Being a boss is more than having a high IQ or academic

qualifications, he points out. It is about having "the intellectual flexibility to look at things from different points of view, together with the social skills and ability to handle people."[10]

Linda Stoker has been in the training business for more than 15 years. She is a qualified trainer and runs her own company, Dow Stoker Training Associates, which organizes courses for women at different levels of ability. Some courses are sponsored by the Manpower Training Commission. They include

> *'Men are conditioned to think "I must" and women to think "I can't".'*

a full-time 'Women into Management' course, directed at women wishing to return to managerial posts, or at "the PA who has been doing the boss's job but not getting the recognition she deserves and would now like an opportunity to step into the boss's shoes."

The courses are designed to give women back the confidence and motivation to pursue the areas of interest that will best fulfil their individual talents.

Participants take part in interviews on video, an exercise in body language in which their self-confidence (or lack of it) is revealed in posture, mode of dress and general demeanour.

Women suffer from a lack of self-worth, says Stoker. "Society tells us right from birth that we are second-best. In theory we have equal opportunities, but in practice these are a bit of a joke."

The courses are, primarily, about teaching women to value themselves. They are also about giving women skills and knowledge so that they are not dependent. "We need to find out what is stopping women from achieving, what triggers their patterns of behaviour, and to get them to discharge their anger and pain. We need to find out what kind of things have happened to them to create this low self-esteem."

Any blocks or hangups can be dealt with via simple counselling: "Most people's distress is only just below the surface."

Theatre director **Susan Todd** questions the whole notion of a career ladder for women and agrees with Germaine Greer's statement that 'women don't want careers, they want life'.

"I think women tend to be quite tangential in their interests. They go where they feel impelled by an interest or passion rather than always thinking 'The next step I should take is *this*'.

At a certain stage I became passionately interested in women's writing and so I went sideways into putting quite a lot of energy into doing that kind of work. It led me off the career ladder that I was then on, because once you've become identified with feminist work (as I certainly have), it is then assumed that you don't want to do Shakespeare, which of course I *do* – and that you are somehow threatening or criticizing because you want to promote women's work.

I notice that younger women directors tend to disavow feminism, which I find very sad."

Actress **Josette Simon** has found sexism to be as much of a problem as racism, because of the preponderance of male directors, some of whom still tend to regard actresses in terms of trivial stereotypes.

"A lot of men don't know how to talk to or deal with women. I don't agree that women directors are always better for an actress. You can have conflicts of a different kind. Generally, though, there is greater empathy between you."

Most actors have no recognized career ladder, but now that she is a rising star, Josette finds she has more say about the way to interpret a part. An actor's power is measured by the size and scope of roles. "The bigger and better the role you play, the more say you are given, because there is more responsibility on your shoulders. It is all to do with how much power you have."

Her big break came when she joined the RSC, one of the first black actresses to play Shakespeare there. The audience responded warmly and were totally accepting.

"Not one single person batted an eyelid. It was a novelty at first, but the theatre is so much about suspending disbelief that this particular aspect of it – playing a person in 16th century England – is no big deal, and the only reason it appears to be unusual is that it isn't done often enough.

People in this business are quick to pigeonhole you. You are a 'redheaded Irish girl', or a 'black actress'. It makes me mad. . . . I am an actress who happens to be black.

I am not pretending I am not black, or that this doesn't present problems, but I don't allow myself to dwell on it. I don't let it get in the way. . . ."

She is loath to see herself as some kind of banner-waving pioneer. "I prefer to teach – to prove – by example. That speaks for itself. It's a case of 'Look at me and learn from me'."

—*'I* didn't arrive in the party political arena by the traditional route. Had I done so, I would never have arrived.*'*—

Meanwhile, back in the real world, it's a buyer's market, and while employers will insist they are only interested in the best person for the job, in practice you are still up against the prevailing ethos of 'Why waste time training a woman when she will only leave and have babies?'

Women are still seen by men and male institutions as a bad investment. In a male-oriented environment (and you can't get much more male-oriented than the House of Commons) such ideas are common currency. Although women are a majority of the population (52 per cent), they are represented by a paltry six per cent of female MPs, presided over by the Chief Queen Bee herself, Margaret Hilda Thatcher. Not a single woman is in her Cabinet.

The 41 women MPs returned to Parliament in the 1987 general election is an all-time record, and almost double the number of those elected in 1983 – but still nothing to boast about. The numbers of women in the House of Commons are fewer than in other European countries and the United States, where women's participation in government is much greater. In the Soviet Union women number nearly one third of 1,500 MPs at the Supreme Soviet of the USSR.

In the United Kingdom the system of selection committees and long, unsocial hours is heavily weighted against women. The Labour Party seems to be trying to redress the balance. It proposes a Ministry for Women (headed by MP Jo Richardson) which would aim, among other things, to help free women of domestic responsibilities that prevented them from being politically active.

Harriet Harman, MP for Peckham since 1982, feels passionately about the imbalance and the archaic way in which Parliament is structured to suit the needs of men.

The role of an MP is "a role which emphasizes qualities which are traditionally regarded as male (forceful, self-promoting), and qualities which are traditionally regarded as good qualities in *women* (being sensitive as well as forceful, flexible as well as knowing when to put your foot down, good as part of a team), are not highly valued and rewarded in the selection process for *any* party. So it does tend to be about individuals elbowing everyone else out of the way and saying 'I'm the greatest', and I think it makes for an unbalanced Parliamentary team.

The route into politics is an endurance test in that it doesn't allow for balancing domestic and work responsibilities. I didn't arrive in the party political arena by the traditional route. Had I done so, I would never have arrived.

The normal route is often years as party secretary at local level, then perhaps as a local councillor, then standing in unsafe seats in farflung corners of the country where you are not likely to get elected. It is impossibly difficult for women for a whole load of reasons – mainly because of the sustained exclusive commitment."

Harriet Harman became an MP via a base in progressive causes and her involvement in the women's movement. While she was legal officer of the NCCL she had a high public profile and was arguing the case for more women in Parliament, believing that "Parliament was not a very representative democracy if it was a bunch of middle-aged men making decisions which affected women's lives. . . . It was at a time when the Labour movement was beginning seriously to feel uncomfortable about a party which, policy-wise, was becoming committed to equal opportunities, yet itself was so male dominated."

She applied to Peckham and got selected in October 1982 to a virtually all-male PLP (Parliamentary Labour Party). She felt 'incredibly isolated'. She was also pregnant. Her baby was born in the first week of February 1983.

"The general election of June 1983 was earlier than it need have been. I had planned that my baby would be at least six months old before I became an MP and had hoped therefore to have conquered some of the foothills of motherhood before the foothills of Parliament! As it was, I was a brand new MP and mother at the same time.

It was harrowing, but it was difficult to work out whether I was being harrowed by being a new and different *style* of MP (because I had come from a different part of the Labour Movement), or how much of it was the general frying of your brain which you encounter with the role of motherhood.

I hadn't a clue what I was getting into. It's impossible to predict. I mean, I was just *me*, pregnant. The whole thing of giving birth was terribly overwhelming – and so is being an MP. I didn't sleep a great deal. . . .

I tried to make as many cover arrangements as I could. I

hadn't worked out how to share the responsibility. I hadn't worked out what was compulsory in terms of the general *footslogging* of Parliamentary work and did more than I needed

— ' *There is an attitude of hysteria towards a baby anywhere near Parliament.* '—

to do. There are unwritten rules in Parliament: you can either endear yourself, or offend people. You have to learn by trial and error, which is very time-consuming and I didn't have any time. Like I was voting on the Friday on some special transport issue and I had Harry on the Saturday. I could have made some sort of cover arrangement but didn't realize it at the time. Because the PLP isn't run by people who know the exhaustion of pregnancy and having a new baby, no one was going out of their way to say 'This is how you might try and work it'. I had to work it out for myself.

There is an attitude of hysteria towards a baby anywhere near Parliament. When I went to vote on the GLC Abolition Bill, Joe was only nine days old, but I thought it was such an important constituency bill that I could just take him in , vote and go out again. Somebody reported to the Sergeant-at-Arms that I'd taken the baby through the Division Lobby. I hadn't . . . but the Chief Whip had to investigate. It was ridiculous . . . There you are with this soft little baby in a world of rather degenerate power-broking.

It's difficult wrestling with a small baby and thinking positively about strategies for future political action. I recognize that the two don't blend together, but it shouldn't create hysteria in the ranks.

Anyway, the last place any self-respecting baby would want to be is in the Palace of Westminster where everything is designed to make it feel excluded, unwanted and uncomfortable."

As a woman, you have to sell yourself really hard in order to convince an employer that you are as fit and capable as the next *man* and that your genital makeup will not hamper you in your work. Discrimination is often a case of blatant double standards. As Roger Bennett points out: "Male assessors might value in women certain characteristics – supportiveness, overt sexuality, maternalism – that are not only irrelevant to most

> *'You have to sell yourself really hard in order to convince an employer that you are as fit and capable as the next* man . . . *'*

management jobs but which also influence men's interpretations of observed female behaviour. If, for example, he considers women to be 'emotional', he will tend to notice emotional aspects of a woman's behaviour – while ignoring it in men." He goes on: "Prejudices are easily formed; most male senior managers have wives who cook and clean for them and secretaries who type their letters and make their tea. They encounter women where they are not expected to exert initiative or assume command.

Add to this media stereotyping of women as dependent, narcissistic creatures, devoted entirely to attracting and caring for men, and it is not surprising that so many male senior managers object to female leadership."[11]

At job interviews try to deflect the line of questioning that dwells on your domestic arrangements and how you will cope if your children are sick. No *man* is ever asked this. You should respond politely but firmly saying that, of course, you have a contingency plan reserved for such eventualities (and make sure that you do).

In the early part of 1987 women applying for teaching jobs in Bedfordshire complained about sexist interviews in which they were quizzed about their private lives. Single women were asked if they intended to marry and have a family. Married applicants were asked if they planned to have more children and who was to look after them. 'Are you on the Pill?' and 'How would an attractive woman like you cope with boys?' were other questions these women faced. Women who did not admit to being on the Pill found their promotion prospects blocked.

The situation was revealed during a survey by a branch of the National Union of Teachers to assess whether the county's equal opportunities policy was working. Clearly it was *not* and the council has since written to head teachers instructing them to honour the policy.

Linda Stoker believes that managements need to move with the changing cultural patterns of the eighties. Back in the fifties, the managerial style was one of reward and punishment: 'mostly punishment'. This squared with the post-war disciplinarian system in schools. Today's pupils are far less restricted, and the business environment, in turn, is changing its approach to 'assertive persuasion – *urging* people to do things rather than telling them'.

Some companies have moved even further, to a situation of 'participation and trust', letting their employees get on with the job and asking them how they think it should be tackled.

"People will no longer just take instructions and obey them. Women question more than men do, because they have been held back for so long. If they have been at home, they have enjoyed more autonomy. You are your own boss at home, and suddenly you have to adjust to working for somebody else."

3

Staying There

POWER WITH RESPONSIBILITY

I n her book, *How to Survive From Nine to Five*, Jilly Cooper paints an amusing picture of the traditional office hierarchy, in which the executive is depicted as chief idiot and procrastinator. "The executive has nothing to do except decide what is to be done, tell someone to do it, listen to reasons why they shouldn't do it, or why it should be done differently, and think up a crushing and conclusive reply. A week later he will follow up to see the thing has been done, discover it has not been done, ask why it hasn't been done, and listen to excuses from the person who didn't do it."[12]

Note the continual use of the pronoun 'he' – less, one suspects, from any syntactical convenience than the writer's assumption that executives were exclusively male. Clearly, there are lessons here for women about how *not* to use power!

Women should not feel compelled to copy men and male methods. They should resist the urge to act like clone men. There are still precious few female role models in high status jobs, but it's important to try and develop your own individual brand of authority, your own approach to the job. How?

Well, for a start, women tend to be more perceptive and

intuitive than men. These are priceless assets which can be usefully deployed and capitalized on in the business world. Communication is the essence of all effective relationships, and it makes sense that a person's performance in the workplace can be enhanced by constructive, diplomatic guidance and support from the top.

Joanna Foster, who heads the Pepperell Unit, the equal opportunities division of the Industrial Society, believes that women's intuition makes them excellent communicators.

"In organizations with fairly traditional management and hierarchical structures, women do seem to bring a far more collaborative way of managing the workplace. They are very good listeners and *involve* people in what is happening much more than a lot of men do. They are good at developing people's individual needs."

This view is echoed by Natasha Josefowitz, who claims that women are skilled at 'process observation', that is, interpreting not only the content of a message but *how* it is being put across. "We see things going on that many men are unaware of. We pick up discomforts, anxieties, fears and angers and often respond to them instinctively. . . . Similarly, we expect men to pick up our emotional cues and respond with understanding. When they do not we label them unfeeling, not realizing that they simply did not perceive what we, in their place, would have seen."[13]

Certainly, it pays to practise a little psychology when you are a boss. In his book, *Habits* (Why you do what you do), John Nicholson says that the application of psychological principles to management "can help to make working a pleasanter and more productive occupation for all concerned."[14] One of Nicholson's rules of thumb for managers is to find ways of creating a climate of openness and improved human relations – and who could argue with that? It was *male* managers he had in mind because in 1977, when the book was first published, senior women managers were an even rarer breed than they are today. Indeed, he wrote at the time that there was "too little information about the performance of women as managers to say whether they are more likely to succeed by adopting the behaviour of successful male managers, or by using some other style."[15]

Data about the performance of women managers is still fairly thin on the ground, and in his book, *Men and Women* (How Different Are They?), published nearly a decade later, one of the key questions Nicholson explores is 'Why do men continue to hold most of the positions in power in public life?'

> *'Management style is a very personal thing and what is right for one person, may be utterly wrong or inappropriate for another.'*

His findings show that although men and women are equally motivated and self-valuing, women have less confidence than men in their ability to perform a task (and in the end result).

While accepting that two world wars enabled many women to enjoy their first taste of work which carried responsibility and prestige, he believes the significance of this fact is sometimes exaggerated. "Nearly four out of ten women in Britain were already working before the 1914–18 war. Indeed, in 1911, they accounted for nearly one in five of all white-collar managers and administrators, a degree of power-sharing which took them nearly 70 years to re-establish! Any gains they made in the years of the Great War were lost when peace was restored."[16]

In examining what holds women back in the eighties, he cites the unequal division of domestic labour. Most women still have to split their energies between job and home, while a man is generally free to pursue his own ambition unfettered. Conclusion: women have neither the time nor energy to compete for the top jobs.

According to management experts, those women who *do* compete generally work harder and are better qualified but do not reach senior managerial positions as easily as men because they are not pushy or upfront enough.

However, management style is a very personal thing and what is right for one person, irrespective of gender, may be utterly wrong or inappropriate for another. The case studies in this book represent a broad spectrum of women, each with her own distinctive approach and tactics.

Some women believe that gender is irrelevant, regarding themselves in an almost asexual fashion. Anxious not to be thought 'soft', these women have internalized masculine values. They act tough, yet at the same time they cultivate an ultra-feminine appearance and demeanour.

They believe in reward on the basis of merit and discount any notion of prejudice or lack of opportunities for women.

Vivien Padwick, Managing Director of Vivair, openly admits to being *pro* sex discrimination. Why? She believes the law has bent too far in women's favour. "Employers now are hesitant to take women on because if anything goes wrong the firm is unable to dismiss them."

Neither she nor *Marie Jennings*, Director, Development, P.R.C.A., is averse to the idea of using her femininity – "as long as one maintains a sense of fairness about it and doesn't try to get away with blue murder," remarks Ms Jennings.

Jean Wadlow, Managing Director, Wadlow Grosvenor International, says she has always tried to look immaculate and to take extra trouble with her appearance. "If a woman hasn't got pride in herself she can't have pride in her job. ... The really big piece of advice is to be good at what you are doing and, if you can, to give yourself the competitive edge over men. Get that extra mark in exams. It's nice to enjoy being a girl and looking good, but unless you know what you are doing and are good at it, you won't get the respect and admiration from the *world*, let alone from men."

Other women deliberately dissociate themselves from traditional masculine values and strategies, and have evolved new ways of working. These women are exploiting *female* values. They may believe in positive discrimination. However, few would dream of using their feminine wiles to achieve their ends. No casting couch hassles for them.

Those who distance themselves most from male methods often involve themselves in women's co-operatives and collectives, and there are many successful examples of these, from office services and videos to removals and furniture-makers.

Katharine Whitehorn, Journalist, "There are those for whom being a woman is either irrelevant or a drawback, and those for whom being a woman is their speciality, and when I went to the *Observer* I came into that (latter) category because I was then writing for women *as a woman* – writing about things like tying up your hems with safety pins. . . . I was cashing in on being a woman.

A few women can do that – actresses playing female parts, or women in fashion. Being a woman is part of what they have to offer, whereas when it comes to jobs in the City, I would argue that the men entirely overestimate the extent to which the job is *neutral*. What they mean by neutral is, nine times out of ten, *masculine*, and they are seeing whether you measure up to it."

Whatever field you are in, choose the style of working that is best for *you* – and for the company. Whatever style you opt for, as a woman you must expect to be judged more harshly than a man, and to receive more brickbats than bouquets – generally from insecure or envious male colleagues with a personal axe to grind.

One man who is pushing for more women in top jobs is Bryan Nicholson, former Chairman of the Manpower Services Commission. At a 'Women on the Board' conference organized by the Institute of Directors in October 1986, he paid tribute to women bosses: "The average female boss in Britain is better at her job than the average male boss. I can't point to any research to support that statement, but it is inevitably true. What makes it inevitable is the fact that the promotion system is so heavily stacked against women that they *have* to be better to beat it."

Sentiments (and, hopefully, more than mere lip service) that are endorsed by virtually all our case studies.

Hilary Sears, of Carré Orban's executive search company, believes that attitudes to the idea of women in director-level appointments are progressing, albeit slowly. Women are still largely invisible in high-status jobs and when Sears sounds out a client ('Can a woman do this job?') the reply has usually been tentative, 'Yes, but we – and our customers – would feel more *comfortable* with a man.'

These days, the response from clients tends to be: 'If you present us with a really brilliant woman we shall be happy to see her'. 'Brilliant' is the operative word.

To get the best out of people, you must establish an atmosphere of mutual respect from day one. Without respect, most relationships – whether personal or professional – are destined to founder. Like teachers struggling to keep order in the classroom, start as you mean to go on. Try above all to be

— '*The promotion system is so heavily stacked against women that they* have *to be better to beat it.* ' —

consistent in your actions and attitudes, so that others know what to expect from you.

Assertiveness is the key here. **Tessa Blackstone**, Master, Birkbeck College: "I'm a fairly assertive person, and for that reason some people may label me aggressive. It is sometimes hard to get the balance right. I think men find that, too, although I suspect that women will be criticized rather more often when they get it slightly wrong.

In much of my working life I haven't had a *major* management role, except when I was in the ILEA (Inner London Education Authority), where there was a fairly big hierarchical bureaucracy in operation. I was in charge of about 750 people in eight branches of the authority.

I'm sure that because there have been times when I felt frustrated or angry about failure to make progress in some

— '*A* manager should be able to tell someone when something is wrong without bruising an ego in the process . . . ' —

way, I have tended to be over-assertive. If you are in a position of responsibility, or playing a leadership role, you also need to be aware of the effect you are having on your junior staff. You sometimes forget that you have this position of authority and that you can be a bit frightening to more junior people . . . and I suspect that I, like a lot of other people, do sometimes forget that."

In the early days of her career, it was humour above all that helped **Linda Agran** to be assertive and to win respect. She is a naturally outgoing, ebullient woman who feels that offering encouragement is vital to the continuance of good working relations.

"I find that men – everybody – responds to encouragement, to the *positive* side of whatever they are doing. Too many people tend to criticize and point out faults. This is necessary at times, but the other side of that is that you must praise where praise is due. A lot of bosses tend to forget this and to assume that people *should* do well all the time, but the moment a mistake is made they point it out to them – and I can't do that."

In her philosophy of 'People Management', American cosmetics tycoon Mary Kay Ash says that praise makes people respond 'as a thirsty plant responds to water'.[17] Feedback is an essential component of good management. It is the only way in which we can develop and learn from our mistakes.

Human beings do not always take kindly to being *told* if they have slipped up, and you should always aim to cushion the bad news with some practical advice or guidance on how a person's work performance may be rectified. *Positive* feedback. Negative feedback kills enthusiasm stone dead, and without enthusiasm, productivity will wither and die. Motivation is meaningless without it. Be direct, cut the waffle and come to the point.

You don't have to act like a maverick, like 'one of the boys'. You don't have to be brutal about it. "A manager should be able to tell someone when something is wrong without bruising an ego in the process" (Mary Kay Ash).[18] Absolutely. A caring disposition is not a sign of weakness or a cop-out. A gentle, sympathetic manner need not detract from the knowledge that you are in charge.

And never, ever, reprimand anyone in public, however heinous the deed. It is the height of arrogance to give a subordinate a dressing-down in front of their workmates. Such a demeaning, demoralizing experience will be seen, at best, as a sign of some deep psychological flaw in your character, and at worst, it will brand you as a tyrant or she-dragon.

All you need to do is to take the person on one side for a quiet word. Point out diplomatically where you think they are going wrong and why you are disappointed with their work or a particular task they have completed. Give them a second chance, and if things do not improve within a reasonable space of time (have a deadline in mind) you may have to take the situation further.

Whatever the problem (bad timekeeping, perhaps, or a one-off task performed badly), nip it in the bud. The longer it is allowed to continue, the harder it will be to remedy it. One person's poor performance can upset the whole team and lower morale. Most people respond well to constructive criticism, as long as it is delivered in a non-aggressive way.

One of the hardest, yet most important, lessons we can learn is to give – and receive – criticism gracefully. We should be neither dictatorial nor submissive. Women especially are vulnerable to feelings of low self-esteem. We are inclined to blame ourselves if things go wrong. Men tend to blame outside influences, the other fellow, the boss, anything and anyone rather than looking to their own inadequacies.

Carol Wilson stresses the need for consensus. "I think it's a good philosophy, both in your personal life and career, to always try to keep your longterm objective in view. It's like if you are in a marriage and you want your marriage to last. Your instinct might be to have a row, and instead you think longterm: 'What do I want out of this?' Then you actually find a way to say something to someone and make them feel good

> '*Your instinct might be to have a row, and instead you think longterm: "What do I want out of this?" Then you actually find a way to say something to someone and make them feel good . . .*'

about it, instead of shouting and making them feel bad. I apply that in my work life now. I will try to find something I can say that is good about someone.

You temper your words. You must always try to get to see other people's point of view, and keep in vision what you are trying to achieve. You don't want to fall out with people.

Women are always afraid that no one will take notice of them. They are constantly put down and afraid that they won't have the authority to deal with people. But they shouldn't worry about it.

At first I was worried about taking people on and running a department. I thought no one would listen to me. It is just the way that women are brought up. But if you have the power to give someone money or a deal, to hire and fire, you will automatically get the respect – you don't have to *win* respect.

When I found I had the authority to sign groups, I thought: 'Who's going to want to sign to *me*? I'm a girl'. Remember, this was the mid-70s, there were no other women doing my kind of work. I discovered that if I was going out and saying: 'Right. I'll give you ten grand', there wasn't a murmur. They realized they were talking to someone who had the power to give them a deal.

That was the real eye-opener for me, and after that I never allowed any of those obstacles to stand in my way, even when I could see people reacting, thinking: 'Can't take any notice of her – she's a girl'. It didn't affect me any more because I knew that if you are in a strong enough position they do accept you in the end."

Ten years ago, there were few women in senior posts in newspapers and magazines. A fair number on the lower and middle rungs of the career ladder, but at the top a (female) void. Now, the picture has changed radically. In May 1987, Fleet Street appointed its first woman editor Lori Miles. Ex-editor of *Chat*, she edited the *London Evening News*, and over the past couple of years more than a dozen women have taken up high executive positions in the national Press.

One of the newspaper industry's new female élite is **Jane Reed**, Managing Editor of *Today*: "You need good health, perseverance, the ability to go on when you want to cry with tiredness, a sense of humour, and a thoroughly good grounding in the basics so that you can talk with confidence about almost everything and not have to spend time circumnavigating problems because you don't know how to tackle them.

I don't know whether I'm any different from a man in my approach. I delegate and am assertive when I need to be. Most people act from a standpoint of *surviving* because, if you are required to ask other people to do things you have to make damned sure they do them, and if that requires you to be assertive, then you should be assertive! You just get on and use whatever qualities you have to use in order to get the job done.

What's interesting is that the things I have learned over the previous 15 years still hold good. In other words, sound management structures are an absolute pre-requisite for anything which you are going to do. However small the structure is, it has got to be there. We didn't have it to start with on this paper and that's why an awful lot of things went wrong, but all the lessons I'd learned in my years in management I found I could call on finally.

The management's business is to make as good a working environment as possible, within the budget, for everybody else. Managers are servants in many ways. They may direct things but they also serve the working people and I think that you can't stop for a minute remembering that."

Another woman appointee to a top-notch newspaper job, is **Genevieve Cooper**, Deputy Editor of the *London Evening Standard*. "I am not by nature assertive or pushy, and no one is more surprised than I am to have got here. This job is particularly good for me. I've become much more confident and sure of myself. When you are in a position of some power, you find that people do defer to you, and so when you become editor, deputy editor or whatever, you start to behave like one. It's almost by default.

I think it's got to the point where women *are* treated like men. If they do the job well they'll go far. If they don't, they won't. . . .

From what I've seen, men are as good at taking assertiveness from other people as women are. They are no more difficult about it. Everybody wants somebody who is good to get on with – honest, hardworking and stimulating company, irrespective of gender.

I've had as many problems from women as from men, for various reasons to do with my personality rather than sexism.

We work so hard all day that we don't get much time for office politics. We don't hang around in corners gossiping. That's when office politics happens – in offices where there's nothing to do."

She feels lucky to be a part of the recent elevation of women in Fleet Street. "Women have become a stronger economic force, and therefore, advertisers want to appeal to them more than ever before, and that is why newspapers want to employ them. That, combined with the fact that women do work very hard. I think women are by nature more perfectionist in their work than men, more conscientious and devoted in some ways.

— ' *Sound management structures are an absolute pre-requisite for anything which you are going to do. However small the structure is . . .* ,* —

But once they've got these opportunities, they should just get on with their jobs and do them as well as they can without being too bloody self-important. There are a lot of women in positions of authority who take themselves too seriously, going around saying: 'I'm an executive and therefore I have to behave in this *executive* manner', and being generally rather boring to be with.

If they keep a sense of humour, and authority, they will be fine and men will forget they are women."

Market research company director, **Ann Burdus** agrees: "The important thing is not to get carried away by who you are but to concentrate on what you are doing and to do it to the best of your ability. Once people get overcome by their own status, they will become very inefficient."

Before beginning her career in market research, Ann Burdus trained as a clinical psychologist. She then went to a top advertising agency (now Ogilvy and Mather) which had its own in-house market research company. It was at a time when it was becoming fashionable for agencies to employ psychologists.

"Motivation and attitude research had a very high profile, so I joined a young, dynamic team and got more and more interested in the application of research to advertising.

I came from a rather behavioural school of psychology, and what I found most useful was the way you were taught to approach and analyse problems until you get to a point where you can handle them. Part of my degree was in philosophy and I have found elementary logic to be helpful.

If you work in mental health, as I have, you develop a slight detachment from problems, which I think helps. Plus an empathy with people. I get angry with people much less than many others I know. I don't find situations so frustrating because I have learned to accept everyone's oddities. It goes back to my days as a clinical psychologist in a big mental hospital, when a patient could tell you the most outrageous things and you'd say: 'Mmm, isn't that interesting!' – you know? – because sometimes they were *true*, and so you never formed a judgement if a patient said something terrible had happened to her.

So later on, when your colleagues tell you outrageous things, you tend to say: 'How interesting!' and take it in your stride.

If it is something personal against *me*, I think that I respond in exactly the same way. One does try to say to oneself: '*Why* does he behave in that way?'

I've frequently felt like exploding – like *striking* them! But I have found it a very useful *tool* in management to very rarely lose my temper so that when I *do*, it is effective.

The other thing is that, on the whole, irrational behaviour is excused less in women than in men, unless they are at the really sharp end of creativity when it's expected of you, whatever your sex. But a woman in management has to be very careful about using irrational behaviour, otherwise she is just confirming all men's worst prejudices."

'The important thing is not to get carried away by who you are. Once people get overcome by their own status, they will become very inefficient.'

Carey Labovitch, Editor and Publisher, still finds it difficult to reprimand people "because I consider everybody who works here as being on the same wavelength as myself. Most are in their early to mid-twenties and I do find it quite hard relating (in a boss-employee way) to people in the same age group as me, because I haven't been employed anywhere else where I've seen a hierarchy work. I've had to develop that myself.

I'm probably a bit too soft. In a way, it's very character-building because under normal circumstances I'd get very cross and in a temper, and then I realize that you have to be very firm and calm and point out what has been done wrong and *why* it's wrong, rather than just tell someone off completely.

I have nothing to do with the day-to-day production of the

magazines any more. I can sit back and let other people take care of them. Yes, I go around telling people what to do if I'm not happy with them, and I do delegate certain responsibilities, yet all the time I'm thinking ahead – to next year and the year after, to what we are doing in terms of promotion, and constantly getting a buzz going on all the titles."

Susan Todd, Theatre Director: "Like most women who seek a place for themselves within a traditionally male field, and also a very conservative one, I have felt very *besieged*. I think that is often a matter of personality. Some people are more sensitive to pressure than others. I get deeply distressed about how certain circumstances can alter a person. I see a lot of directors, men and women, who are perfectly nice people and whose ideas I respect, becoming ego-driven monsters.

In a way, the director is always invading other people's space, and unless you have interesting, strong relationships with the actors working with you, that sort of invasion can become a monstrous thing and not the creative dialogue which you always hope that it's going to be.

I know for a fact (because others tell you!) there have been moments – where the needs of the situation demand speed, fast decisions to be made and so on – when I, also, have been monstrous.

At the time you feel so *driven*. Also, it's to do with circumstances. You are the only person who knows exactly what all the problems are. You are the one person in possession of the facts about all areas of difficulty. Actors are not. You are, therefore, juggling all these different areas and hoping the problems won't collide with one another and bring about disaster. You are where the buck starts.

I find it rather too easy to be aggressively assertive and I have to control that. I find it very easy to impose my opinions, both by a certain shoddy eloquence and by force of personality or force of will, and for much too long I have allowed that to be the case. As a director you need to be able to leave space for other people's feelings and opinions. Because I'm a woman I'm over-assertive and over-aggressive. I'm less able to relax, to allow things to remain unresolved, than perhaps a very mature male director might.

I've often solved my problems about lack of confidence by bullshitting, by being far too ready to express an opinion, and it won't do.

Men, on the whole, are more relaxed than women. They have an easy way of filling up space and time with their thoughts and ideas, whether they are any good or not. There is a kind of ease and relaxation about the way they do that, because their place in the world is legitimated. Masculinity

> *'A woman in management has to be very careful about using irrational behaviour, otherwise she is just confirming all men's worst prejudices.'*

isn't questioned. It is femininity which is the estranged, the unspoken or *outside* quality.

Women are often very edgy about their status, about how a director feels about them, and when you are working with a large group of women, as I often have done, it can be difficult. I think that is underlain in a very profound way by women's relationship to the figure of the mother. All of us, men and women alike, are terrified by the power of the mother, and we all at some level want to destroy that power. A woman in power is an ambivalent and ambiguous emblem, and if you are a woman in power, you carry this *projection* at an unconscious level."

Beverly Anderson has worked in senior positions in education and broadcasting, and on balance she has found education to be the more interesting and rewarding profession.

"As a class teacher and as a head, I have been accustomed to having a lot of control over my working life. As a TV presenter, I was expected to take responsibility for decisions made by other people – for programmes which I hadn't actually been involved in constructing. The presenter, as I saw it, is merely the face of someone else's decision.

There are *some* programmes with which I've been associated that I've enjoyed and feel proud of. *Black On Black* (Channel 4) and *A Parents Guide to Secondary Education* (BBC1) were both, in their different ways, extremely satisfying to do. The public treated me in a very friendly and equal way, and it was fun learning new skills. I'm not saying I wouldn't do it again, but as a way of earning a living it isn't satisfying enough.

The trouble with broadcasting is that it's not systematic. You can, if you are lucky, catch somebody's eye, but it's a very fickle business. If you do something competently you can't assume there will be a follow-on from that. There is no sequence. You may stay there for ten years, or two minutes.

In education I've been able steadily to prove myself. As a teacher I have a say, I make decisions about what I teach and how I teach it, I check on whether people are learning what I have taught them, I have a relationship with them which is personal and continuous, and for me, those are more important satisfactions than I found in being a TV presenter."

However, she is aware that as a black woman appearing in a white, male-dominated media, she was a role model for many of the black community in Britain.

"It seemed beneficial that somebody like me was there – for them – and that was the pleasure I got from doing *Black On Black*.

I'm aware that the freedom I had in Jamaica a lot of black people in this country don't have. I grew up in a society where black people ran everything, so that I knew that I was free to choose any career I wanted, and I realize that in this country those messages are not there for black kids.

So, if by being on TV and looking successful I made black

English kids think: 'Perhaps I can do that as well', that's a very useful function.

I've never been a victim of racism, and I think that's to do with my advantages – the fact that I was born in a part of Jamaican society which was over-privileged, and went into a part of American society which was also extremely privileged.

> — '*I*'*ve often solved my problems about lack of confidence by bullshitting, and it won't do.* , —

I tend not to notice prejudice, because I don't need to worry about it, and I've always been employed as a teacher on my *abilities. . . .*"

Get to know your team as individuals: their strengths and weaknesses, temperaments and limitations. Take a personal interest in their wellbeing. Women are particularly adept at this as they are good at interacting with others in a non-paternalistic way.

A prolonged period of therapy has helped **Susan Todd** to improve her interacting skills, and also to be aware of deep-seated feelings like envy and competitiveness: "Bringing those feelings to consciousness is an important part of one's work on oneself because, as a director, if you don't know about most of your darker feelings you won't be able to deal with problems that arise in a text, or conflicts that arise between yourself and actors."

You should learn to stimulate the enthusiasm of your team, as it is only through constant, topped-up motivation that you can be sure of reaping the best results and keeping morale high.

High morale means better productivity and a happy team, and this is an obvious asset to the company. There is nothing more fatal than a bored or disenchanted employee. It can only reflect badly on you as supervisor or team leader/manager. So sort out any petty bones of contention before they build up into terminal grievances, spreading rumbles of discontent throughout the department.

Use your intuition. If you sense that an employee has a genuine problem, encourage her or him to share it with you. It might be something totally unconnected with work which is, nevertheless, spilling over into, and affecting, that person's working day.

> *Subordinates appreciate most a manager who trusts them, gives them responsibilities, and allows them to take initiative and make decisions.*

Don't jump to conclusions. A reduced work output and more time off might occasionally be a sign of skiving. More often than not, it could point to either trouble at work or at home. Trouble at work could be caused by a clash of personalities in the department, which might require some internal changes for the sake of team harmony; trouble at home could be caused by domestic friction such as an illness in the family, or a pending divorce.

Gauge the situation. If she or he seems preoccupied, or starts taking large chunks of sick leave for no obvious *physical* reason, try to find out what is wrong – gently and discreetly, firmly but fairly. Choose your moment but don't force the issue (see Chapter 6 on coping with stress problems).

Suggest a meeting with the staff counsellor if you have one. More and more companies are recognizing the value of counselling skills in the workplace to ease problems of over-stressed staff.

So, unless someone is widely known or suspected to be a skiver (in which case warnings and/or marching orders may already have been given), allow them the benefit of the doubt. Hear *their* side of the story.

Vary people's workloads as much as possible. Offer them fresh challenges. Without playing the nanny role, encourage them to feed you with ideas and to work on their own initiative. Use your imagination. Put yourself in their shoes, and remember how *you* felt when you were struggling to get ahead. If you had a hard time on the way up, that is no excuse to make others suffer, so don't vent your pent-up anger and frustration on those a few rungs below you. You will only court hostility and such tactics will do nothing for your reputation.

Learn to delegate. Besides easing the pressure on *you*, a willingness to delegate is a sign of personal and professional maturity, a sign that you are confident, in control and coping. "Delegation is not abdication. You remain accountable for the results in your department when you report to your boss. Let your subordinates be accountable for their performance if you give them the responsibility.

Besides, subordinates appreciate most a manager who trusts them, gives them responsibilities, and allows them to take initiative and make decisions. You will head a team that has everyone pulling strongly in the same direction."[19]

Delegation denotes confidence in your subordinates' efficiency, their ability to deliver. It is not an excuse for laziness. You can't sit back and let other heads roll for *your* misdemeanours. Like it or not, you will ultimately have to carry the can for your team's mistakes.

Vivien Padwick buys her staff books on delegation. "Our ploy here is that management's job is to make themselves redundant. I have the philosophy that you must make yourself dispensable, but with the sheer *volume* of work. . . . I came to the point where I never had enough people to help me, so I don't think delegation has been my problem at all!"

There should be clear demarcation lines between your duties and those of your subordinates. This is essential to any team work. There should also be a certain flexibility of operation which allows you the freedom to offload tasks. Be sure to brief members of your team carefully so that each person knows what she or he is expected to do.

Hold a meeting to discuss the issues. Regular meetings are a useful way of maintaining contact with staff, both those below you and above you. Meetings help you to keep tabs on what is happening in the rest of the department and to clear the air if there are any grievances.

When you attend any meeting don't be afraid to make your voice heard – and your presence felt. This is even more important when you are in a minority of one – like Jenny Abramsky, BBC radio news and current affairs boss and the most senior woman in BBC radio or television journalism. Ms Abramsky has long been accustomed to being a lone female voice in meetings. At 40, she is the only woman to have edited Radio Four's top three news programmes: *PM, The World At One* and *Today*.

There are only 12 women (and 167 men) at her top management level in the BBC, an increase of six since the corporation's report on equality was published in 1985. (Monica Sims, former director of programmes for BBC Radio, was commissioned to write a report on the dearth of women in senior positions in the BBC, the reasons for this and what could be done to rectify it.) At the next level down, which includes senior producers, there are 87 women and 771 men. No less than 87 per cent of secretaries and clerical workers are female.

Whatever your position in the hierarchy, get your point across as clearly and concisely as you can, and don't let anyone interrupt you. Many women still find it an ordeal to stand up and speak in public. They tend to be reticent in their delivery, and men take advantage of this. Don't let them!

There is an art to speaking and acting authoritatively. According to management consultant Lee Bryce, it is about 'positive personal power', which is about getting things done, being able to walk into a room in such a way that people know you are to be taken seriously.

Bryce, who is organizing assertiveness courses for women (run by the British Institute of Management), explains: "We help women to see that power is not a dirty word: it has responsibilities as well as advantages, and women can learn to

— '*Management's job is to make themselves redundant. I have the philosophy that you must make yourself dispensable, but with the sheer* volume *of* work. . . . ' —

use it in a way that fits in with their personality and without becoming macho."[20]

In other words, it's not so much what you do or say, it's the way that you communicate with others and the force of your personality that counts.

Delegation is about decision-making, a major facet of the management role. The very act of delegating a task amounts to a decision. *You* are the yardstick against which members of your team operate. They look to you for guidance. You lead by example. It is *your* decision (to accomplish a piece of work or to complete a contract, for example) which shapes and affects *their* decision-making.

Once you make a decision, stick to it. There is nothing more irritating than a vacillating boss, and as a woman, you will find plenty of 'I told you so' critics only too ready to use your hesitation as a stick to beat you with.

Know your limitations: don't bite off more than you can chew. Learn to say 'No'. Don't agree to a course of action unless you are ninety-nine per cent certain you can see it through to fruition. It is all very fine to be creative, an ideas

> *'I still maintain the overall view and control of direction, so I can at any point say: "I don't think we should go along there . . . I think we should do this." . . .'*

person, but as someone once said, an idea is no more a novel than a germ is an attack of measles.

We are all familiar with the type of person who is all talk and no action, who – throwing caution to the winds – trumpets his or her latest magnificent discovery to everyone within earshot. This kind of reckless boasting immediately arouses *my* suspicions. I ask myself: 'Will it ever get off the ground and on to the drawing board? or is it just a glorious fantasy destined to remain locked forever in the other person's imagination?'

I am not advocating false modesty. That can be as ridiculous and pointless as constant boasting. However, adequate follow-up of ideas and decisions is crucial if you wish to avoid a chaotic department and a disaffected workforce.

Fashion designer **Betty Jackson** likes to be involved at every level in the day-to-day running of her company, and this means careful monitoring and follow-up of ideas and suggestions generated by her and members of her team.

"I think our limited success is due to team work, more than anything – gathering people around you who are interested in the product and in the process of getting that product across, and who are willing to back you on both a professional and personal basis.

It's important to be able to continue to give direction to people, but if they then can carry it out as well, that's really marvellous. I have a limited amount of time that I can spend on anything, and at one time I found myself ending up doing lots of things in a mediocre fashion. When I placed other people to do those things, and they reported back to me a synopsis version of what had gone on, then it worked much better.

I still maintain the overall view and control of direction, so I can at any point say: 'I don't think we should go along *there* . . . I think we should do *this*.' . . ."

As director of the largest market research company in Europe and probably the fourth largest in the world, **Ann Burdus** recognizes the importance of proper follow-up and feedback. She has a long and distinguished record of high status managerial positions. When she was head of research (for Europe) at McCann International she used to spend about 47 per cent of her time travelling, though less impulsively than some of her male colleagues.

"We had a lot of executives who, when there was a problem, used to leap on a plane and only then start to work out what they were going to do, and I believe a few hours' thought in your own office can solve quite a bit."

On the way up, when you were seeking out opportunities for your own personal advancement, taking the odd risk showed initiative. Now that you yourself are a boss, you cannot afford to be too impetuous. You must be sensitive to the possible consequences of a bad or mishandled decision. Resist the urge to jump the gun. Listen first to the voice of caution inside your head.

Whatever your decision, remember to involve other people,

and learn to convey a clear, unambiguous message of your intent. As in the best managed *social* situations, the wrong message can lead to misunderstandings and misinterpretations. "Nothing demotivates people more than the frustration of not being asked or involved in the decisions that affect them. Over a period of time this makes them antagonistic to *any* new plans. The time and energy wasted in repairing the damage caused by lack of consultation and involvement is far greater and less fruitful than spending time thoughtfully at an earlier stage."[21]

The moment you are assigned even one typist, you become a boss. It's rather like becoming a parent, in that you suddenly, overnight, acquire responsibility for someone else besides yourself.

Even given the range of management training schemes on offer, few of use are trained to be leaders. Most people, in the final analysis, are tossed in at the deep end and left to swim, sink or flounder. Make sure you don't fritter away too much time floundering and, if in doubt, don't be too proud to ask *your* boss for a helping hand.

4

Sexism

‹——————◆——————›

DEALING WITH DISCRIMINATION

‹——————◆——————›

Masculine hostility towards women in top jobs is ingrained and badly needs to be removed. The worlds of business, commerce and industry are still, to a large extent, bastions of male chauvinism which seek to perpetuate the status quo and to keep women out. They have shown a studied indifference towards the whole concept of equal opportunities when, traditionally, women have supplied them with a cheap, compliant labour force. Understandably, men have a vested interest in keeping it that way.

Any woman with a spark of initiative faces a constant struggle to overcome sexist barriers. Some men may actively provoke confrontation, in a deliberate attempt to undermine a woman's authority and morale. Or they may simply, privately, deem her too emotional, weak or soft to compete in *their* territory and dismiss her abilities in the workplace.

Such attitudes are part of the institutionalized sexism that abounds, the kind of mentality that for 37 years prevented women from actually buying drinks at the bar of that well-used Fleet Sreet watering-hole, El Vino's – until November 1982, when Anna Coote and Tess Gill won a High Court ruling against the wine bar. (Newspaper columnist Miles Kington neatly described the place as El Time Warp.)

It was a victory for principle although, even now, few females can be glimpsed jockeying for position among the sea of suits and smoke. Hardly surprising when you consider that the lifting of the ban was accepted with such ill grace by the manager, Paul Bracken, who not only declined to shake hands with Coote and Gill but promptly tried to get both women banned altogether on the grounds that they would be troublemakers.

On an individual level, some men's sexism manifests itself in various forms of sexual harassment (see Chapter 6). Others behave, whether or not they realize it, in a highly patronizing fashion towards women, and in many ways this can be a tougher response to tackle, as several of my interviewees have discovered.

Linda Agran: "Actual discrimination is more subtle, which is why it's more difficult. I mean, it's quite easy to deal with someone who says: 'The only reason I'm employing you is that I thought you'd be handy on the side'. It's harder to deal with men who are perfectly *reasonable* and listen to your little problems and yet you know that you are never going to get any higher in the company.

Most *men* I've worked for have never made a programme, and I know women who are really well suited to go to the top but who never have and never will, because they are not given the opportunities. And, what's more, the Government takes no action to make companies feel awkward about this.

As for sexist remarks – if I'm in a good mood, I just giggle. If I'm in a bad mood, I just mutter under my breath. I don't really want to know if the liftman thinks I look good today. I don't want to be called 'love'. If you tell men that, they will either say to each other: 'Well, she's obviously a dyke', or 'That's the trouble with women – probably her time of the month'. I resent it. . . ."

When *Barbara Switzer* applied for her first job as a full-time union official, she walked out of the interview: "I just blew it. I had a bit of an argument about the terms in which the conditions of employment were couched. They were extremely sexist, with all male language and so on, and I said: 'You really ought to have thought about that before you sent me a document like this', and that started me off on the wrong foot!

> *It's harder to deal with men who are perfectly reasonable and listen to your little problems and yet you know that you are never going to get any higher in the company.*

I suppose I hadn't set my heart on getting the job, but was determined to try for it. The interview was before a committee of sixteen men and there was no dialogue as such. They treat you fairly but it's still quite an ordeal to go through. I stuck it for a short while, then said: 'I have nothing more to say to you' and left.

I applied again six months later. Full-time officials' jobs don't come up that often, but at that time the union was growing rapidly, particularly among women, and I went for the interview and succeeded. The conditions of employment document had been changed. They had taken my criticisms on board and revised it."

Katharine Whitehorn: "The one time that I was really *mortified* was on the old Spectator. We were a chummy little clique: Brian Inglis, Alan Brien, Cyril Ray, Bernard Levin. Inglis left and Ian Hamilton came as editor just before Bernard Levin left. I was told there was to be a farewell lunch at the Garrick for Bernard and I turned up in the board room in my best red suit at about 12.15 pm. At about 12.35 Ian Hamilton said: 'Well, I'm sorry, Katharine, we're off now', and I said: 'Yes, that's what I'm here for'. He said: 'Don't be silly. It's an all-male lunch'.

The others hadn't realized, either – because the Garrick did allow women as guests in the *evenings*. They hadn't thought about it and they were furious. They took me out to a nearby hotel and poured champagne into me, and Bernard was forty minutes late for his own farewell lunch. We were all extremely cross about it.

But I got my own back on that bastard. We were all leaving anyway, because the proprietor said he was standing for Parliament as a Conservative, but I stayed longer than most of them because I was being sued for something and I didn't want to get stuck with paying my own costs. As soon as the lawsuit was over I was off, and Ian very badly wanted me to stay. He offered me all sorts of inducements, but after what had happened nothing in the world would have persuaded me to stay, and it was a positive pleasure saying 'no' to him."

Carol Wilson: "While I was working for Virgin Music publishers one of my writers had co-written a song for a Roxy Music album. The manager of Roxy rang me and said: 'Your writer can't have a credit on this album. It's going to be credited to our publishing company – okay, *dear*?' He thought I was inexperienced and that he could walk all over me.

I said: 'No, it's not okay. We want our credit, unless you can give me a very good reason why not.' I stood my ground. He hit the roof and said: 'You're a good copyright girl but you know nothing about management.' Very demeaning! I was furious at the time, but we've made it up since.

In the early days I found that men would be incredibly rude to me. They'd insult me and try to make me angry, because I was a woman. There came a point, after I had a couple of hits, when I began to shout back at them to get my own way. It worked in the short-term but over the years I realized that it was very bad for long-term relationships.

It still happens – sexist insults and all that stuff . . . I've got a great store of cutting remarks I can make where necessary.

There are still a lot of men who don't like seeing women out at work (especially in senior jobs) and they are constantly testing you out, but with most of them I build a relationship and work with them and there is no problem. There is no point in getting bogged down in fights, because no one wins."

Others, like **Marie Jennings**, are less affected by the vagaries of sexism, wherever it may occur: "It's difficult for a woman to go into a conference with 200 men. I was the speaker at the first CBI conference for John Methven on industry. It's difficult to go into that situation, but if you want to make a statement in that kind of debate and you are the only woman there, it's easier for you in a sense because some of the old

> **'***I** don't really want to know if the liftman thinks I look good today. If you tell men that, they will either say to each other. "Well, she's obviously a dyke", or "That's the trouble with women – probably her time of the month".***'***

courtesies still prevail. People were kind to me. I could have found it intimidating had I allowed myself to, but I didn't.

I wouldn't say that men *try* to be patronizing. I just don't register that sort of behaviour. If I noticed it, I'd get uptight.

I think women have the best of both worlds and I'm not against that at all. I'm married, I have a family. I've been married before and been through all the traumas of divorce, looking after and bringing up a child.

I'd much rather see it in terms of recognizing that there are *differences*. It's my positive decision to be in business, so if I have to suffer a bit for it it doesn't worry me. It's my decision. If I'd wanted to be the little woman sitting at home, I'd have been in that role – and probably an absolute pain to my husband and family!

There are still pockets of discrimination, but I think that it is much better to be positive rather than to draw attention to them all the time. Better to demonstrate by excellence rather than grizzling about this thing or that thing being unfair."

> *'Better to demonstrate by excellence rather than grizzling about this thing or that thing being unfair.'*

Jean Wadlow thinks that women make problems if they play on the sexism question. Her advice? "Forget about it. Just get treated as an equal. . . . Just fight, that's all. You can't give up. You've got to be persistent. Don't let them get away with it. Play them at their own game."

Ann Burdus: "I think it really doesn't do to get agitated all the time about sexist behaviour but to choose your moment. Sometimes it can be the most kindly people. A super man I used to work with at Interpublic in New York would make a speech to the assembled gathering of (often) two women among numerous men, and before using some strong language he would *apologize* to the women. I took him on one side once and said: 'Either you shouldn't be saying what you're saying, or you shouldn't apologize' – because the apology (in such a situation) is a terrible form of discrimination.

He was staggered when I pointed it out, and said: 'Yes, of course I realize. . . .' But choose your moment. I think women become great bores when they go on and on about these things.

I've also schooled myself to feel sorry for people who carry prejudice of any kind, and therefore, my immediate reaction to an impossible colleague is not anger but *pity*."

During her stint as a traffic manager at Willesden, **Sarah Kendall** kept finding copies of porn magazines in her internal post. She coped with it by "chucking the stuff in the bin and just getting on with the job.

To an extent, it is a deliberate wind-up and I wasn't that keen on pursuing it. I was fairly certain who was responsible, but if I'd said anything it would not have helped. It would not have been taken seriously. After about six months, it stopped.

When I left, my colleagues said: 'It's been really nice working with you' . . . 'I never thought I'd like working with a woman' . . . 'You've done a good job'. That almost justified the aggro I'd gone through.

I have had an abundance of comments from other, more senior managers and also more junior members of staff – like 'Women shouldn't work on the railways. It's a man's industry' . . . Or 'You won't be worried about promotion because you'll be getting married soon' . . . Or 'Are you courting?'

It's not so bad now. I have proved myself, though I still have to keep proving myself to an extent.

I feel quite strongly that in management jobs on the railways each woman can do her own pioneering work. It's easier for another woman going to an area like Willesden now, as I have paved the way."

Barbara Switzer has always been in a male environment: "I was at a co-educational school and I had three brothers, so I was well used to it. I took an engineering apprenticeship, which was quite unusual at the time. I learned to cope, and survived. That experience made it easier for me to go into trade union circles, a male-dominated area. But I've had to fight the competition, of course, and that means fighting hard for your point of view. I'm accused of being *sharp*. . . . Lots of adjectives are used against a woman for doing things that would be described quite differently if done by a man.

I do argue strongly and vociferously for my point of view, and that's described as being aggressive when all I am doing is arguing just as strongly as my colleagues do for *their* point of view, but it's seen as something quite different, simply because other people have hangups about women.

I keep on saying, when people go on about this kind of thing, that they have the problem, not me.

It frustrates me more than upsets me. Sometimes I feel as if I'm knocking my head on a wall. They don't seem to understand what it is that's wrong or dismiss complaints as emotional reaction, but I don't see it as a major problem. It's just an occupational hazard.

TASS has a good reputation for its attitude to women, but you are often patronized. Some people patronize you because they intend to. Others patronize you because they do not

> *'I'm accused of being sharp. . . . Lots of adjectives are used against a woman for doing things that would be described quite differently if done by a man.'*

know that is what they are doing, they do not realize that is what the effect is, and some of the most progressive people can do that.

I think the trade union movement has been prepared to

listen and try to resolve some of the problems. It's an uphill task for them because they are having to tackle their own prejudices – the women too, because *they* have certain entrenched ideas as well. It's not surprising when we see what they've been fed for generations. It's difficult to get some of the women to change the way they see their own role, but in the main it's getting men to look at themselves (because the unions were set up by men for men and there's an awful lot of tradition to break down), and to look at the structures and see if they are conducive to women's involvement.

When I was an apprentice on the shop floor, some of the male apprentices used to say to me: 'You know, you're never going to get married. Fellows won't want to marry a woman who earns more than they do!'

You sometimes hear careless remarks or sexist comments. It is important to deal with them. Sometimes you can't react at the time because of the circumstances. You want to, but it would be inappropriate. You just have to bite your tongue and get hold of the people responsible afterwards and say: 'Now look here, that's not good enough. Just cut it out and don't do it again.' They say: 'What did I do?' They, quite genuinely, had no idea that they were causing offence.

I think that people do make an effort now – committed people. Others just want to stir it and be unpleasant, but in the main, union leaderships have taken it on board.

At the end of the day you can get a lot of respect and credibility by getting on with the job and fighting in your corner. I think that's so essential – just to argue it out and not be put off."

Beverly Anderson: "There *is* a lot of sexism about in education. When a new head of department is being thought of, I have heard people carelessly saying, even in institutions like the one in which I work, 'What we need is a young man in his thirties' – even though most of the staff in primary education are women! And, of course, the people who are saying that are men. There is still a tradition in education that men run the thing and women *make* it run.

In my particular case, I have been lucky. For most of my working life I have been treated as an equal by men. So, when I do occasionally come up against sexism, I'm surprised by it, but sexual equality is by no means established. It's an issue I care a lot about and am trying systematically to do something about, because a lot of women are still held back by sexism, sometimes at an unconscious level."

Most of the women who talked to me did not have clearcut goals from a young age. Others, however, decided early on in life that they wished to pursue a particular path. These women were drawn to some of the most conspicuously masculine preserves, areas where sexist attitudes are so deeply embedded they need a proverbial scalpel to root them out.

In most faculties of medicine, for instance, women are still grossly under-represented. In general surgery there are only six women to 957 men. Out of the total of nearly three thousand surgeons in Britain, women number 66.

Britain's only woman neurosurgeon is **Carys Bannister**, whose special interest is in children's neurosurgery. She is a Consultant Neurosurgeon at Booth Hall Children's Hospital, Manchester, and North Manchester General Hospital, and also Honorary Lecturer in Paediatric Neurosurgery at the University of Manchester School of Medicine.

As a child she wanted to be a doctor, and after taking A levels she set her sights on becoming a surgeon. It was the mixture of the human and the practical that appealed to her.

"It never crossed my mind that there might be discrimination. I had feelings of inadequacy as a person but not as a woman."

But when she started going for interviews at medical schools she soon learned to keep her surgical aspirations to herself. "People thought it was a totally unrealistic career for a girl. Even as a 17-year-old it was not the thing to say and would have done no good to my prospects at all."

She was accepted at Charing Cross Medical School, where she qualified with Honours in Surgery, reflecting her interests. At first she was undecided as to which branch of surgery to try.

A year or so at Birmingham Accident Hospital opened her eyes a great deal. She came into contact with her first head injury cases and her interest in neurosurgery grew.

But she was up against a wall of prejudice about women's suitability for surgical posts, particularly in this most male-dominated of specialities.

The main pitfall early in her career was getting the right jobs. "When it became obvious to everybody that I was a serious contender for neurosurgical work, committees would get frightened. All committees discuss candidates behind closed doors. Their attitude was: 'But of course you won't stick it'. They felt they would be investing time and money into you, only for you to leave, get married and fall by the wayside. Other women had been in training and dropped out. It was suggested to me that I might wear out. This made me more determined."

> *'I saw male colleagues who were less experienced and less senior being appointed. I was faced with the prospect of not succeeding ...'*

After a number of 'house' jobs she spent more than eight years as Neurosurgical Senior Registrar at Leeds General Infirmary. During this time she applied for numerous consultant posts, but without success. The surgical hierarchy is pyramid-shaped "and the competition becomes hotter as you move up the pyramid. There are a lot of house jobs, fewer registrar jobs and even fewer senior registrar jobs. I saw male colleagues who were less experienced and less senior being appointed.

I felt I was being overlooked. It got to the point of being quite frightening. I was faced with the prospect of not succeeding, and yet I was absolutely sure that neurosurgery was what I wanted to do.

I wasn't aware of being treated differently when I was actually in a post and working. The crunch seemed to be when I went to interviews and was constantly asked if I was strong enough to do the job – sometimes by people who *knew* that I was and who had been in close enough contact to see me working, yet they never asked me at the time whether I needed help!"

One male colleague, a careers adviser, told her while she was at Leeds General Infirmary to think again about neurosurgery.

— *'I wasn't aware of being treated differently when I was actually in a post and working. The crunch seemed to be when I went to interviews . . .'* —

She thanked him very much for his uninvited advice. He replied: 'Talking to you is like hitting your head against a brick wall.'

"One problem is that all this sort of advice tends to make women in medicine rather aggressive. When one is told: 'You will not succeed', this is hard to take. I think I am less aggressive now than I used to be. One finds other ways to fight, to achieve the things one wants to achieve. I teach students. I have outpatients' sessions, and we talk after the clinic over a cup of coffee. I value those times and they are very informal.

I don't feel I am some sort of maverick, though I am

disappointed there are not other women coming into neuro-surgery or into senior registrar posts in neurosurgery. ...Women need encouragement. They need to see more role models, otherwise the rumour goes around that they will not make it.

The numbers of women in any surgical field are remarkably small, even those where you might have expected the numbers to be high (e.g. gynaecology, paediatrics). Many young women students tell me they would like to do surgery but few believe they will do it. By the time they have finished medical school they have become disheartened.

I want to shake them and say: 'Don't be put off'. . . . The sad thing is that it requires a level of aggression which is not needed in men, because men are encouraged to get on right from the start. Looking around, I see women doing surgery who are super-aggressive."

When she was much younger, the junior doctors, a little 'put out' at being told what to do by a young woman, were quite rude to her. "But as I've gained seniority, they know that their careers depend on my assessment of them. They have to mind their P's and Q's with me as I write their references. This is a universal medical joke."

To be a successful neurosurgeon, stamina and persistence are prime requisites. "We are still very much on the edge of what is possible. You can have success or failure. Things can and do go wrong. Failure is pretty awful but you have to take that situation not as a blow but as a challenge: 'How can we get around the problem? . . . How can we ensure that it doesn't happen again?'

It can be very heady stuff – people rushing around and telling you how marvellous you are. You might sometimes get a little overtaken by it, but a few shocks around the corner can soon bring you down to earth.

At the time you are operating it is very absorbing. A lot of work is done down the microscope. It's a very small, shut-in world. You need to prepare yourself. It is essential to be 'psyched up' beforehand and a little bit of adrenalin certainly improves the sharpness of your reactions. Our operations are long – rarely less than four hours."

She is unmarried. "I decided that I couldn't do two jobs badly. I would feel terribly split and that I was not doing either job well."

Her work, in any case, is so deeply involving that it leaves little time or energy for outside pursuits.

"Most of my life has been spent in medicine, much of it locked up inside hospitals. I find it strange to be outside that environment. One lives in a big group of people in a very close community and it becomes a way of life."

At home she spends a lot of time preparing lectures or research work, and she is often on call.

There is a high stress factor, especially the night before a major operation. "You may spend some time sitting and thinking about it. It takes its toll but it's not something I can't cope with.

The whole of the brain is a challenge. We know so little about it. The *drive* that keeps me going is the thought that in one's own small way one can advance the study of the brain and how it operates."

About 35 per cent of consultant haematologists are women, which makes it less male dominated than most other medical specialities, largely due to a history of more regular hours. However, like Carys Bannister, haematologist **Sally Davies** has found sexism to be deep-rooted within the medical hierarchy.

"I was discussing this with a woman senior registrar, and we agreed that a new male consultant in the hospital is being watched far less than I was when I started. I've been a consultant for about three years and people still watch me. One senior consultant is trying to limit the amount of clinical work I do. It's because I'm a young woman that he feels so threatened. He's tried every line. He's tried patronizing me and that didn't work. He's now tried appealing to an even more senior physician to get me to curtail my activities – to cut down my present number of patients to about a third.

Medical politics works on power bases and caucuses and which committees you are on. I've been developing my own power base. I've been elected to the hospital management board (as one of the two consultants on it). I'm the youngest they've ever had, and the only woman, and I have access to a lot of information that otherwise wouldn't come my way, so that I can try and alter decisions in a way that *I* want them. I can use my influence."

On a more mundane, day-to-day level, her response to condescending male colleagues is generally to hold her tongue. "I find it counter-productive to argue, because a woman who

— ' *The only means of getting my way is to be terribly reasonable, quiet, calm, nice. This generates a lot of stress and tension, so I have to go off and lose that somehow . . .* '

is strongly assertive is assumed by most men to be aggressive, hysterical, over-the-top. The only means of getting my way is to be terribly reasonable, quiet, calm, nice. This generates a lot of stress and tension, so I have to go off and lose that somehow – by aerobics classes, skiing and tennis."

In Sally Davies' first year at medical school, only a tenth of the students were women. Both her parents are academics and her father played a very egalitarian role in the home. Her sister is a barrister and her young brother is a consultant radiologist.

"Medicine was the one thing no one else in the family had done . . . and at medical school the women were much brighter and did much better, so it was an advantage being a woman in terms of exams and getting one's first job.

I gave up medicine for four years after I married. My first husband was in the diplomatic service and we went straight off to Spain, where I tried to be a diplomat's wife, which did not suit at all. I did not like being 'Mrs Somebody' and not having my own salary.

Then we came back, he was in the Foreign Office over here and I went back into medicine. I was much more motivated. I was lucky, I got the first job I applied for – in paediatrics."

She spent a year working for a 'superb' consultant and studied for more exams at the same time. Her marriage

> '*For most of my working life I have been treated as an equal by men. So, when I do occasionally come up against sexism, I'm surprised by it, but sexual equality is by no means established.*'

collapsed under the strain. She decided to change to another field of medicine where the hours were more civilized.

"Haematology was just beginning to blossom as a subject. I went in at the right time. It is one of the biggest growth specialities, and one of the most developing and fascinating ones. We now cure 70 per cent of children with leukaemia. My work is 50 per cent malignancies, 50 per cent sickle cell disease, an inherited anaemia of blacks. I work in Brent, where 65 per cent of the population is ethnic minority, and we have the biggest clinic of sickle cell disease in the country."

She heads a team of about 25 in her department, which has a

budget running into hundreds of thousands of pounds. She still finds difficulty in delegating. "It goes back to the idea that if you do it yourself it will be better done. However, I'm improving!

Women have a lot to bring to medicine. Their care of the patients is generally much more human and the patients quite like women doctors. A lot of the men find they can relate to you differently from male doctors.

We play more of a counselling role. With male doctors, it tends to be: 'How are you today? . . . Oh, your blood pressure is up. Take this tablet', whereas I sit there and the patient may say: 'Well I'm having stress because they might be making me redundant at work'.

Women are also less scared of giving physical contact to the dying patient than men are."

For Sally Davies, job satisfaction lies in "recognition of work achieved; getting the patients better; building a good department that is getting an excellent name around the country; and trying to improve the lot of people who don't have a very good education and can't work the system for themselves as well as they need to."

In the legal profession women now account for nearly half the entrants. Once qualified, however, they are far less visible than their male counterparts. In 1985/6 women made up 46.5 per cent of new articled clerks, but only about a quarter of women solicitors are partners in firms, as against 60 per cent of men.

The figures for women barristers are even less encouraging. Only 13 per cent of barristers are women, and the number of women QCs is a little over three per cent. Even so, things have clearly improved for women since 1976 when, in her book, *The Bar On Trial*, barrister Helena Kennedy revealed that most chambers had no women at all and some even operated a 'no women' policy.

In 1984 Ms Kennedy, whose special interest is in civil liberties, set up her own chambers with a male lawyer friend, with an express commitment to sexual and racial equality.

Women, she claims, "have changed the style of advocacy very much for the better. . . . Where men tended to specialize in pomp and display, women have been far more concerned with communicating, in a lower key way, with juries. And, like naturalism in the theatre, that has caught on and become the popular way now."[22]

For the judiciary, the picture is still a bleak one for women, who make up about one in 27 judges. It is one of the most extreme examples of the old boy network in action. Judge James Pickles, dubbed the 'turbulent judge' for his frequent clashes with the former Lord Chancellor, Lord Hailsham, has publicly denounced the complacency, conservatism and conformity of a system which gives white, middle-class men with an Oxbridge background a head start.

In the prison service there are just six women governors out of a total of around 125. Among them is **Muriel Allen**, governor of Britain's only male lifers' prison: Kingston Prison, Portsmouth. She was appointed to the job in April 1982, the first-ever woman governor of a male prison (four more women have since been appointed as governors of other male establishments).

"To me", says Miss Allen, "it didn't feel at all strange walking in here to take over, though I had to be sensitive to the fact that it was very novel to the staff and prisoners.

I sensed no hostility, but I did sense an intense *curiosity* because of the importance of my role and how it would affect either the working lives of the staff, or the institutional life of the inmates.

Various inmates approached me wanting to know what sort of changes I would bring about. Both prisoners and staff are far too sensible to think it meant lace curtains and flowers everywhere, but they were interested – and not hostile in any sense."

On her first day she recalls 'an almost obsessive concern' about how she was to be addressed. Was it to be Governor, Miss Allen, Madam, or Boss? They settled for Governor or Miss Allen.

The real initiation came with her first prison adjudication. If a man has offended against known rules and regulations and the officer has charged him with that offence, the governor must deal with it in a formal way. "It's rather like a mini–court, based on the principles of English justice, with witnesses called

> *I sensed no hostility, but I did sense an intense curiosity because of the importance of my role and how it would affect either the working lives of the staff, or the institutional life of the inmates.*

if appropriate. I've dealt with adjudications before, but here it seemed to me the whole prison waited with bated breath as to how this woman was going to deal with the situation. Would I be soft or accommodating?

When you've worked in institutions for years, you can *smell* the atmosphere. Your senses are attuned to the institutional responses and I picked this up early in the day.

I dealt with the matter and I learned afterwards that word went round like wildfire: 'No change. Just the same as before'. They relaxed. I was going to be neither punitive, nor lenient."

For the inmates, the appearance of a woman governor had a certain novelty value. "I think what they were all telling me, without using any words, was their experiences with women to date. Their reactions to me as a woman spoke volumes."

A high proportion of lifers at Portsmouth have been charged with offences such as rape, arson or aggravated burglary, but the majority are serving sentences for murder and the victim is almost invariably female. "Therefore, it was doubly important to me, coming here as governor, to show some sort of role model if I was going to be of any social skills value."

The staff's initial response to her was 'a slight sense of awe'. It was more: 'She's come from Head Office' than 'This is a woman'.

There are 140 inmates (one man one cell) and 130 staff, from

> *'There will always be those women who prefer to blaze a lone trail to the top and are proud of the fact that they did it their way. It is those women who help to keep sexism alive and flourishing.'*

prison officers to support services to maintenance staff and workshop instructors and supervisors.

Miss Allen's deputy is a man, but the administration officer and an assistant governor are women. There are women teachers, typists, clerical support staff and cleaners . . . but not cooks and bakers.

"You'd have the devil's own job anywhere in the prison service to get women to be cooks and bakers. When I worked at Head Office in London before coming here, I was sent for one day by our director who said: 'We are extremely puzzled. Why can't we attract women into the service to be cooks and bakers? I would have thought they were ideal jobs for women. We can't *understand* . . .'

I waited till he'd finished his speech. Then I said: 'I'm very glad you invited me to answer this question, Sir. Women join the (prison) service to get *out* of their kitchens!' There was shock, recognition! . . ."

A person can become governor either the traditional way, as an officer moving through the ranks, or *sideways*, straight into an assistant governor role – as Muriel Allen did.

She traces her sense of commitment back to her roots in South London, where she was born, third in a family of ten children (six boys, four girls). It was the kind of set-up which quickly taught her to stand on her own two feet and compete for attention.

"It is still fairly rare for a woman to get into the prison service and I can only focus it on the war years and the enormous sense of relief I felt that I and my family survived – and the feeling that if one did survive all that, then there had to be some good reason. There was a need to put my life to what might be perceived as some good purpose.

I didn't have any formal education, mostly due to the war years, but also to my dear father's old-fashioned views that education was wasted on women because they would get married and the boys would get the chances."

She left school at 14 and got a job as a junior clerk on the Croydon Advertiser, 'sticking stamps on letters and answering the switchboard'.

Gradually, her sense of vocation grew stronger and more specific. It was the time of certain causes célèbres: the cases involving Craig, Bentley and Ruth Ellis. The prison service attracted her but she kept 'pushing it away' because of her abhorrence of capital punishment.

Meanwhile, in the modern equivalent of a late adolescent rebellion, she went abroad, to France and Scandinavia, working in a biscuit factory, au pairing. She returned to England and applied for a supervisor's position in a girls' remand home. She was accepted, and in time was promoted to deputy superintendent.

In 1964, one month after capital punishment was abolished, she applied to the prison service and was appointed an assistant governor at Holloway where she remained for six years. From there, it was a steady climb up through the ranks, including two years as third-in-command at Durham Prison, her first experience of a male prison, followed by four years at Prison Department HQ in London, and then the biggest challenge of all, her present appointment at Portsmouth.

When it comes to doing the job, she doubts whether either sex has any prerogative, "but I think that male governors and prison officers are more comfortable with the authority role and less comfortable with the caring, compassionate bit. Women governors and staff tend to be the reverse."

'*As a man I have had so many years building power. I now know that I have to withdraw from that position of male power and allow women to take their rightful place in society.*'

She believes the main pitfalls have been more to do with her personality and management style than her gender. "I'm impatient. I have no difficulty at all in clearly seeing a problem and working out how I can achieve the solution. What I cannot bear is getting from A to B.

Early mistakes were in rushing into things bearing in mind that this is a small, quiet prison in which the pace ought to match it. . . . I still have a need to get things done."

She gets frustrated with bureaucratic delays and the kind of attitude that resists change because 'it's always been done this way'.

She finds the job *demanding* rather than stressful. "Responsibility and authority sit very lightly on me. It doesn't upset me when a man comes in fighting mad, spitting with rage and shouting at me. In a way, it calms me. I know that somehow I've got to bring him down, understand why he's in such a rage, see the context of that. . . . To see two men desperately fighting doesn't frighten me. It has the opposite effect. Sometimes I think there's something missing in my make-up that I'm *not* frightened!

I don't ever have a need to control fear. I have this curious absence of it, but I do feel very strongly that fear acts on fear. If aggression and violence are met with fear, they act on it and – it seems to me – produce murder."

As a woman, she has to conceal any personal feelings in her dealing with certain categories of offender, such as rapists. "The professional response comes with experience and professional skills. It doesn't mean that I do not feel shock and a certain revulsion, but when I'm talking to that man and trying to see where he's at and where I hope he will be in time to come, I find no conflict at all in doing that as equably as I do with the next man, who may be a mercy killing.

It is particularly difficult for child offenders and rapists to live in a prison community. I will not have them excluded from it in the way that is perhaps necessary in some other prisons, because I have to help the man to see that unless he can live in *this* community, there is no hope for him out there.

They are not segregated. I believe that Rule 43, which allows me to do that, is necessary on occasions: if the man is in physical danger, I will use it for his own protection. But as I say loud and long, rule 43 is against my religion. The challenge is to grab that problem and deal with it in this community.

I would like to think that it works by personal example and – this is the leadership bit – demonstrating that I make no distinction between one man and another. In the natural order of things, we like some better than others, but the professional bit is to suspend one's judgment."

She admits to finding it more stressful working in a *women's* prison. "Male prisoners adapt much more easily to the prison regime because they are much more used to the group situation – to meeting in pubs, clubs and so forth.

Women, on the other hand, are more individualistic. The focus of the home is theirs and they bitterly resent being taken away from that and not having control over their own lives to the extent they had before. They feel deprived of the role of mother, wife, sister, aunt. A man feels emotionally deprived, but in a different way and almost at one step removed.

Part of the role of staff is to absorb some of those tensions and that can get very stressful indeed. I felt that I'd aged from my experiences in women's establishments. When I came here I felt a sense of liberation. I am freed to get on with the job of being a governor – of managing."

Leadership, of itself, can be quite isolating for women as there are still so few female faces at or near the top of the career escalator. According to recent research, the numbers of women in senior managerial posts has actually declined in the last five years or so.

In many cases, women find their feelings of isolation compounded by sexism. As Lesley Chesterfield, a management trainer involved in equal opportunities training courses, explains: "As the only woman in many work situations I have had to deal with patronizing, dismissive and even downright rude behaviour from men. Like other women, my conditioned response would be either to collude with sexism, ignoring such behaviour by withdrawing, adopting the passive 'feminine' role, or to show my anger and become aggressive and hostile. Either way I increase my isolation – not only from men but also from other women."[23]

She stresses the importance of good support systems in helping to combat sexist attitudes.

In the same article John Langford, another management trainer, comes clean about what many men are often reluctant (or too arrogant) to admit: just how difficult it is to surrender power. "As a man I have had so many years building power, without realizing what I was doing. I now know that I have to withdraw from that position of male power and allow women to take their rightful place in society."

One organization that has achieved a great deal in promoting women's confidence and management potential is the Pepperell Unit, which was set up in 1984 as an arm of the Industrial Society to help companies develop and implement equal opportunities policies. It also encourages women of all ages to cultivate their skills and abilities to the full, and runs courses, conferences and workshops for women considering returning to work – and in schools and universities.

> '*As the only woman in many work situations I have had to deal with patronizing, dismissive and even downright rude behaviour from men.*'

Named after Elizabeth Pepperell, who pioneered the Industrial Society's work with women, the Unit recognizes that equal opportunity is as much to do with men and their attitude to changing roles as it is to do with women's attitudes. The household comprising breadwinner husband, economically inactive wife and two children, once the norm in Britain, has long since been overtaken by the two-income or dual career family.

Women with the tiniest modicum of personal ambition, however, have to be prepared to slot into a man's world as, historically, organizations have been tailored to meet men's needs and way of life. There, at the grassroots, lies the real, practical, daily source of discrimination. No wonder that women who have made it to the top of their professions feel excluded, alienated, even when viewed from below with envy by other women struggling to gain their first tentative toehold on the career ladder.

Parliament, as we have already seen, is a case in point.

Harriet Harman: "Women MPs are not on the same grapevine as men. They are not taken into male caucuses or cliques, which disadvantages them when decisions are made in an informal way.

> — '*Women MPs are not on the same grapevine as men. They are not taken into male caucuses or cliques, which disadvantages them . . .* , —

I feel a different species from them. I do things a different way. My most acute sense of my own difference and distance from my male colleagues, many of whom I have a close and friendly relationship with, is to do with the onset of mother-hood at the same time as my becoming an MP.

I don't feel *disadvantaged* because I don't aspire to be like them. I don't want to get into that club. I want to change the rules of the club. I think it should reflect much more the people it's supposed to represent. I feel that having the preoccupations of a family is not only a great privilege and very rewarding, but actually enhances your political approach because it gives you a sense of perspective, balance and priorities.

I feel *they* – the men – are disadvantaged, by their narrow view of the world. I feel that my view of the world is superior. The only problem is that it's a hopeless minority, and therefore it doesn't impact itself enormously, but if there were loads more women it would refresh and broaden politics."

Susan Todd agrees: "After a very long struggle women are now being accepted into more of the public areas of life. I think the predominantly male Establishment have become embarrassed about the absence of women, because feminists have been hammering it home for a long time, and finally it is bearing fruit. There is a shamefaced acknowledgment that women do indeed have to take part – at the upper levels of management, not just at the middle and lower levels. ... There have always been lots of women theatre administrators, for example, but not women at the level of creative control in film, theatre and television – by which I mean *directors*. ... As a director, you are right at the *face*, at the point at which the artistic product is public, the point at which images are forged. This is immensely potent and exciting. And men, of course, have always wanted to have control of that potent image-making.

I think the presence of more women at the top alters the atmosphere. It's a qualitative difference, and certain sexist attitudes – in casting, for instance – would get laughed out if there were more women involved in that process."

The City, one of the greatest male preserves of all, is a particularly lonely place for women, although more and more women are beginning to make inroads here as directors of broking firms and banks, or in senior positions on trading floors. Lesley Watts, director of the merchant bank, Kleinwort Benson, was a runner-up in the 1987 Veuve Clicquot Young Businesswoman of the Year competition.

The City Women's Network, which organizes regular meetings and newsletters, has a growing membership. Bank manager **Betty Guyatt** (manager of a branch of the Midland Bank in North London) helped set up Women In Banking, and thinks networks are valuable confidence-boosters for women.

"In the early days of Women In Banking we had training sessions about assertiveness and so on, which certainly wouldn't have been available in the bank – and learning about power. Power play is one of the biggest male weapons. At that stage we hadn't identified it as being even an instrument, so if you can go to an organization where you are all women together to learn about these things it's like a revelation.

I think networks were very important in the early stages and also now, as one advances, it's important that women have contacts they can use in the same way that men use their contacts."

There will always be those women who prefer to blaze a lone trail to the top and are proud of the fact that they did it *their* way. 'Anybody can', they cry, like a tired old record, and yet they would be the last people on earth to lend a hand to their struggling sisters coming up behind them. It is those women who help to keep sexism alive and flourishing.

5

Juggling The Priorities

THE TRICKY BALANCING ACT
BETWEEN WORK AND HOME

A t home, your child is sick. At work, a crucial deadline or meeting looms. Which should you put first? An all-too-familiar dilemma to most women who work.

Above all, the woman in business is far more likely than her male counterpart to have to wrestle with two sets of responsibilities: office and home, colleagues and children. Most men take it for granted that somewhere in that separate sphere called Home waits a woman who takes care of children and chores. The higher up the ladder she climbs, the more split her loyalties can become, and the more personal conflict – and guilt – this engenders.

As women, we have learned to switch our thoughts from mundane chores to high-powered conferences to the reading of bedtime stories to our children. While we talk business, we are often thinking: 'What shall we have for dinner tonight?'

Ironically, it is this very ability to wear and balance so many different hats (an obvious asset in the business world) which in practice can work against women, simply because the structures of that world are largely weighted against them.

Marie Jennings: "Women have an inherent management

component. A woman has to manage her own life, home, family. Given the opportunity, women have got the edge over men in terms of management generally."

Women tend to be more organized and better time managers than men. Most men swan along single-mindedly, free to give every ounce of their attention to that compartment of life labelled Work.

Former Manpower Services Commission Chairman Bryan Nicholson acknowledges the extra burden on women in managerial jobs.

"There is evidence that many women managers encounter higher stress levels than their male counterparts, caused by the combined stresses of work and home.

At home, many have reported higher pressure due to conflicts over their career versus their partner's, the running of the home, child rearing and so on, suggesting that female managers are not always getting the support they need from their partners."[24]

In some cases, this is putting it mildly. Failing a social revolution which would compel men to do more than make sympathetic noises, it looks as if women will continue to take the lioness's share of work in the home.

The question of 'Who will look after the children?' is an ongoing one, which involves organization, a certain amount of luck (all the right qualifications and experience won't mean a light unless your nanny/au pair achieves instant and lasting empathy with your children), and *timing*. More and more women are postponing motherhood until their late thirties and even early forties – an age when they are more likely to have established a career niche for themselves. On the whole, this seems a sensible trend. It means that you return to work afterwards with the confidence and self-awareness that comes with maturity. You have a clearer idea of what you want out of life. You have surmounted several rungs of the ladder and earned the respect and kudos that this entails. (You may even make a better mother, too.)

However, as a new mother, you may find this new, dual life

exhilarating but exhausting.

First, there is the sheer energy level needed to fulfil the demands of work and a young baby, perhaps with sleepless nights into the bargain.

> *'Many women managers encounter higher stress levels than their male counterparts, caused by the combined stresses of work and home.'*

Next, there is the problem of child care arrangements. To save yourself unnecessary stress, a reliable back-up service is vital. It's important to get this settled at the outset in order to avoid complications later on. The last thing you want, as you strive to reclaim your place in the company hierarchy, is a lot of angst over catastrophic nannies or au pairs. This is especially true when you are running your own business.

Fashion designer **Betty Jackson** has two children, both under five.

"We have a full-time nanny who's brilliant. We couldn't function without her. She doesn't live in but she comes every day and that's worked very well. Both children wave us off happily in the morning. I'm sure it's alleviated a lot of problems, because we've been so happy with her.

You absolutely have to get that sorted out, even if it costs you the earth – because to be worried about the domestic situation would be a nightmare. It is *so* demanding running your own business in the field that we are in – the competition is so great and people expect so much of you all the time – that if you had those other worries at the back of your mind you couldn't do it. No way."

So – get organized. Shop around and find the most convenient, reliable arrangement for *you*: a plan which will fit in with your routine and lifestyle. Depending on where you live and what facilities are available, this will involve a day nursery, child minder, live-in or daily nanny whose hours conform to your working day and who goes home when *you* do.

The main thing, especially if you work unsocial hours, is to have a familiar face, a constant presence with whom your children can easily identify.

Treat it as a sound business investment. Time spent in advance exploring the options available will be time well spent and energy saved in the longterm. Don't expect your employers to make allowances for any lack of foresight on your part. It's part of the unwritten deal between you and them that you should have ironed out the domestic side of your life before resuming your responsibilities at work.

— *'Most working mothers find there is a conflict, whether it's school holidays, a child's illness, or not going on a training course because it involves evenings or weekends.'* —

If you have a supportive partner, this is the biggest bonus of all. Ideally, it should be a person who respects your right to be successful, someone who is mature and secure enough not to feel threatened by your accomplishments, or by any fame and fortune that might accrue to you. But above all, it should be someone who will acknowledge that household and family duties have to be shared. That if you go home to collect the child or relieve the nanny one day, he will do it the next; that he will rearrange work schedules to cope with the family, as well as you. If he doesn't measure up, or if you find yourselves constantly at loggerheads over trivialities or who-does-what-when, then maybe you should consider trading him in for another, more enlightened model!

Parliament is strewn with broken marriages, a casualty of the long, unsocial hours and peripatetic lifestyle. If your constituency is close to the House of Commons, this is an advantage.

Harriet Harman lives in her Peckham constituency, 'within spitting distance' of Westminster. Her husband, Jack Dromey, is the National Secretary of the Transport and General Workers' Union. They have three children, all under five. The youngest, Amy, was born in January 1987. A live-in nanny called Pat looks after them.

"I'm the main parenting parent. Jack does a lot of the back-up work – washing, shopping, etc. I'm the one who sorts out the schools and makes the arrangements for when I'm not here.

He does make a big contribution to the running of the home, but I take the main responsibility for the children.

Jack has an extremely high-powered, pressurized job in a world that is as exclusively male, as narrow-mindedly pro-work and anti-family as Parliament. Most working mothers find there is a conflict, whether it's school holidays, a child's illness, or not going on a training course because it involves evenings or weekends. . . . There is an inbuilt tension between parenthood and work, and because this is one of my causes, I'm able to speak up for it and be more assertive about how to do things.

Being an MP is an individualistic type of job: you work out your own ways of working. . . . I have quite a tightly organized regime. I tend to come home at the children's teatime, 5.30, for their putting-to-bed, and then I go out again, so I manage to do an 11-hour working day, while spending as much time as possible with the children.

I don't go on Parliamentary delegations to Hong Kong or do tours of Scotland, etc. You can't win the struggle for socialism just going backwards from Peckham to Westminster, but that's all I can manage!

> '*I* remember feeling incredibly guilt-ridden and torn when I first left my son with the childminder. He cried when I left him and cried when I picked him up after work, which was even worse!*'*

I don't engage in either necessary or unnecessary jaunts abroad. I think that provides a fatal flaw in our political representation, as well as providing a dog's life for the spouse. It's the notion that you are too important to spend time at home. There's something wrong with that person, that notion. . . . It doesn't reflect a healthy respect for the importance of being a parent and bringing up the next generation."

PR boss **Marie Jennings** lived in a flat attached to her office in London's Mayfair when her children were small. She has one son of her own, two 'inherited' from a former marriage, and four stepchildren from her present marriage to a globetrotting 'energy and innovating' expert.

She employed a live-in nanny and has always worked throughout her childbearing years, apart from a brief spell at home for the birth of her son.

"At the time I was running a programme for the Berlin

Senate. My gynaecologist was ringing up trying to find out where I was, because I was supposed to be having this baby. I went in and had a Caesarian. I had a pretty rotten time, and she said: 'I have no sympathy for you whatever. You've brought it all on yourself'. She made me feel frightfully guilty. A week or so later I was out and had no problems.

Later on, when I was a director of J. Walter Thompson's PR company, and attitudes were still a bit old-fashioned, I remember a young girl saying to me: 'I think I want to go and have a child'. I said: 'Well, it's the most simple, natural thing in the bloody world. Why should you not?' . . . If a young woman wants to do that, then I, in a situation of employing them, would say 'By all means, off you go and come back when you're ready'.

Doreen Stephens (she was in charge of BBC children's TV) had done a lot of work in relation to this problem of women having children and feeling guilty if they weren't at home. She always told me that women ought to realize that having a family is a very important thing but you also have a requirement to satisfy yourself, and by doing that, in a sense you satisfy the child more. And I do believe that is right.

"With hindsight, I would have spent much more time deciding the sort of person I was, rather than flying by the seat of my pants all the way through.

The tips I'd like somebody to have pointed out to me more when *I* was young, were to know myself more accurately and to know better what I wanted out of life."

Educationist **Tessa Blackstone** has two children, both in higher education – "ostensibly, but not financially, off my hands". Like Marie Jennings, she worked almost continuously throughout their growing-up, returning to work very soon after each birth.

"We were too hard-up initially to afford a nanny. I had my children when I was young and not yet established in a career. I was in my early twenties, and it was therefore a great struggle.

I was still a student when my first child was born. My mother-in-law looked after him for the first year, and after that

I took to him to a childminder. When my daughter was born we employed a girl who had worked in an orphanage for two years. She came in the morning and left in the evening.

After a couple of years we moved and we had a married woman who brought her own 18-month-old child with her, and that worked quite well until my daughter was well established at primary school.

I remember feeling incredibly guilt-ridden and *torn* when I first left my son with the childminder. He cried when I left him and cried when I picked him up after work, which was even worse! Eventually, he did adjust. But I do remember thinking: 'I can't go on with this', but I know that it was right for me to do so. I would have been very frustrated and unhappy as a full-time mother.

Perhaps if I'd been a bit older I'd have taken more time off than I did, but after all, I was doing this in the mid-sixties – before it had become established, as it is now, that women could have children *and* a career, and I therefore felt under great pressure to demonstrate that women could do this without asking for any additional time off, or concessions.

I was in a small vanguard of women at that time who had decided they were not going to be like the women of the fifties who abandoned a life outside home and domesticity for quite a lot of the time . . . and it helped that there were quite a few other women in similar positions whom one was close to.

I was criticized by older relatives, both male and female, and by older colleagues. That in itself put more pressure on me, but I was fairly clear in my own mind that what I was doing was right for *me* and in the end would be right for my children."

In many branches of commerce, industry and other areas of work, the hours are punishingly long. This makes it all the harder for women to synchronize work and home lives effectively, and is a serious bone of contention with many of our interviewees.

Harriet Harman believes that more women will be wooed into the House of Commons only by a change in the 'maleness' of political culture, and by changing the hours of Parliament so that women are not faced with a rigid 'either-or' choice between family and a career in politics.

It's important to re-examine relationships in the home as well. Changing the external structures is not enough. "If a woman still has a hundred per cent responsibility for the home, she won't have much energy and initiative left for making use of that space which has been created outside it.

There are a number of extremely talented women running local authorities or departments of local authorities, handling multi-million pound budgets, who don't put themselves forward for Parliament. Many women aren't prepared to engage in the personal sacrifice which Parliamentary political work has come to mean because it's been fashioned by men. These women are not lacking confidence or ability. They've got too much sense to go into a situation that is so crushingly anti-family life.

— '*Many women aren't prepared to engage in the personal sacrifice which Parliamentary political work has come to mean because it's been fashioned by men.* **'** —

If you come along to a selection committee and say : 'I will travel the world for socialism and not take a holiday for five years', the current prevailing wisdom is that that is a good thing, without saying: 'Just a minute – who's bringing up your children? What about the attributes of *that* person?'"

Tessa Blackstone believes that career women with young families need above all to be well-organized and to be able to fit in a wider range of activities in a normal week than men do. They also have to be willing to make certain sacrifices, particularly when they have small children.

"When my children were young, I had very little free time. We didn't go out or entertain much. Life consisted of work, looking after the children and running the house.

I also think that on the sacrifice front, if women really want to pursue a career successfully, there are times when they'll have to say: 'He must cook his own meal tonight', or 'Somebody else will have to take the children to the swimming baths' because it is quite impossible to do everything. . . .

My husband, now dead, found it easy to identify *intellectually* with feminism and with opportunities for women, and was very committed to that, but in practice, when it came to taking on certain tasks, he found it more difficult. Whilst he was in many ways very good with the children, the actual organizational side did fall on me."

One woman who has always borne the brunt of child care arrangements is **Beverly Anderson**. Like Tessa Blackstone, she has spent most of her working life in education. She is a single mother, who has been married twice.

"Both times I married I expected to take a secondary role and do the traditional thing where my work would be a complement to the man's. My career has taken a number of ups and downs which have reflected that pattern. . . .

As a result, now I am in my forties, I am considerably behind equivalent men – men with the same degree of intelligence, training and experience of running huge institutions. I am a classical woman in the sense that my domestic choices and responsibilities are reflected in my status.

I don't regret it, because it was my choice and I do enjoy my work, but there's no denying the problems of being a woman with a functional uterus! If you wish to use the uterus, then you are at a disadvantage in the world of work.

I stopped working for three years after I became pregnant with Hamish, at which point I was a deputy head. I then had to go back to work as I needed the money and gradually worked my way back up to be a head teacher.

At about that time my working life went through a series of dramatic changes. Shortly before becoming head, I was elected to Oxford City Council. Six months later it became clear to me that I couldn't be a head, mother and councillor all at the same time. When Channel Four invited me to present *Black On Black*, that fitted in very easily with my responsibilities as a mother and a head. The local authority gave me one day off a fortnight to present it.

> — ' *My husband, found it easy to identify* intellectually *with feminism but when it came to taking on certain tasks, he found it more difficult.* , —

I was then living with my second husband, who did most of the childminding while I rushed out and earned the money to support us. He was there with Hamish when I wasn't. It was very strenuous and hard on us all, and my husband found that particular role rather difficult."

She had no additional child care help at that time, partly because they could not afford it, and partly out of personal preference. "We didn't feel it was fair to Hamish. I think on the whole he was better off having two people who were fond of him taking care of him in his own home. But there were times when I would refer to him as a baton. My husband was trying to study. I would steam in and grab the baton, he would hand it to me and steam out . . . so although in some ways it may have been quite hectic for Hamish, I think he was quite secure."

Later, she had to depend on a series of babysitters – and still does. Her back-up arrangements are, she says, rather hit and miss at present. "I have always wanted to have as much of the pleasure of rearing my own child as possible, and I am prepared to put up with rather muddled arrangements in order to do that.

I know other friends who have done it differently. I'm aware that there are a whole range of patterns for doing it and

> *'I feel a responsibility towards younger women, with children, feel a responsibility to prove not only that you can do it but that you needn't have a broken marriage – and if the BBC doesn't let you do that then sod the BBC.'*

the kids seem to turn out equally well. But I didn't want to pay someone else to have the fun. *I* wanted to have the fun!"

Jenny Abramsky is one of the few senior women at the BBC to have successfully combined children with a high-powered and pressurized job. During her interview for the editorship of Radio Four's *Today* programme, she stated her own terms.

"When I said, during my interview, that I must be able to accompany my children to and from school once a week, a sort of *silence* fell ... Afterwards, everyone said I'd probably spoiled any chance I ever had of getting the job."[25]

She was working on *World At One* at the time. When her son was born she took the full 29 weeks' maternity leave but after the next child, a daughter, was born, she was back at work three weeks later.

"I feel a responsibility towards younger women, even more now that I have moved on to a level of responsibility, with children, which not many women in the BBC have reached before. I feel a responsibility to prove not only that you can do it but that you needn't have a broken marriage and you can retain your sanity – and if the BBC doesn't let you do that then sod the BBC."[26]

When **Katharine Whitehorn** first joined the *Observer* as fashion editor in 1960, she combined the job for a year with a weekly column for the *Spectator*. "It was 28 hours a day and my husband complained bitterly because he never saw me. I was doing fashion for two or three years, by which time I was in my mid-thirties and trying to have babies. I had two miscarriages and the doctor said: 'You'll have to calm down or you'll never keep one', so I quit the fashion and started writing the column, which is more or less what I've been doing ever since."

Her husband, crime writer Gavin Lyall, works in a study at the top of the family's home. Living with another writer, Whitehorn admits, can pose its own special stresses.

"It's agony, but also very good because we read each other's stuff and keep each other up to the mark.

But in the sixties Gavin felt obliged to be excessively rude about my work and I was reduced to tears every Wednesday (copy day). I finally said: 'Don't you think you can phrase it a bit more politely?' And he learned to say: 'Kath, this is absolutely fine *but* . . .'– rather than: 'A tenth rate night sub on a provincial would never turn out stuff like this even if drunk'.

Originally, we were on *Picture Post* together and doing the same job. To an extent, it's been easier since we have been doing different things. The difficult bit is that we also do them on different time scales. Anything that goes on for more than a week I consider *long*, whereas Gavin's time scheme is two or three years. So he tends to come off the hook for six months at a time, but I have to keep churning it out.

When the kids were small, there was always plenty of help around. We had a sublime woman called Trudie with us for 17 years. She originally came as a cleaner/housekeeper, then evolved into a daytime nanny – brilliant with babies and like a second mother to them.

We gradually topped that up with more daily help, then living-in mother's help.

I always got them up and nearly always put them to bed, so the power centre stayed *me*."

She is aware of the dangers of trying to keep too many balls in the air. "There have been occasional periods when I've taken on too much and it's resulted in things becoming extremely difficult at home. If you are doing too many things somebody else takes the strain, and the one year it went badly wrong was when I went back into the office and tried to do editing. That was disaster. I had not managed to offload enough of the things I'd already been doing. Gavin was at home and I don't know whether things really fell apart as much as he thought they did, but he got to feel trapped, as if he was a sort of house-sitter, which was psychologically appalling. He was foul to me and I was miserable, and I remember walking up the path thinking: 'I wonder what I've done wrong this time?'

It would be absurd to say there were no difficult patches, but I doubt if they were any worse than the kind of difficulties that occur when a woman sits at home being bored utterly stiff, waiting for hubby to come home and make her feel meaningful."

When **Ann Burdus** first met her present husband about six years ago, she was so busy that when he invited her out to lunch the earliest free date she could manage was six weeks ahead.

He works in financial asset management. He is self-employed, works partly from home, and takes his share of the domestic chores.

Women, Ann Burdus believes, are often possessive of their skills in the home. "It's not just a matter of the husband refusing to do the cooking or whatever. It is the woman taking such pride in the cooking that she won't *let* him, she won't delegate in the way that she would delegate at work!

I do cook, although my husband is a dab hand at making breakfast and there are all sorts of other jobs I am more than happy to give him at home.

— ‘*T*o do the "okay" thing, which is to wait until the children are fifteen and then go back to work, has awful problems too, because by then the chap has got used to you always being there to service him and to his career coming first.*

’ —

He likes going to functions with me. He's also very protective. I tend to protect my private time a lot, so when it comes to asking people to dinner, he does all that. I'm quite happy to cook dinner but I don't like the picking up of the phone beforehand.

You have to plan a bit and use the support services when they are available. I remember the first time I got caterers to do a private cocktail party for me, I was mortified, because I'd been taught that was something you should always do for yourself – and of course, it *isn't*. If you are busy, you get somebody else . . . I learnt a lot of that in New York. In New York you can conduct your whole life from *bed* if you want to, and if you've the resource to do it!"

Not all my interviewees, of course, are married or mothers. According to research carried out in the US in 1982, the 'composite woman senior executive' in large American companies was 46 years old, unmarried and had no children.

More than half of the women who talked to me are single and/or childless. They tended to be no more tenaciously ambitious than those with family ties. In most cases, the decision not to have children was reached only after long and careful thought.

Like most men, they could afford to be more single-minded about achieving their career goals, undistracted by children's ailments or school holidays. This, in turn, made some more prone to workaholism. The difference is that, unlike most men, there is no woman at home ready to 'service' them.

Theatre director **Susan Todd** shares her life with actor Roger Allen, a close and valued friend. "We've worked together, often. He is very successful at the moment and I feel joyful that I can share in that. It works the other way as well: he's pleased when nice things happen to me.

> '*If you choose to have babies you become responsible for another human being, but the way things are arranged at the moment, it is* women *who have to accept the responsibility.*'

The world of theatre is absorbing and, in a way, quite addictive because it has this exciting rhythm of constant new events, new shows. . . . It's very immersing and you can find yourself involved in endless trivial gossiping about the events of the theatre to the exclusion of all else. It's rather cosy, like being part of a tribe."

Managing director *Jean Wadlow* is divorced and lives alone in a mews house in Mayfair, London. A self-confessed workaholic, she can see her office from her bedroom window. It means that she can never really leave her work for long – but then she has no desire to.

She employs a housekeeper, who helps her in the office as well as at home.

She has no children. "I think that is something you have to decide early on. I don't think you can do both successfully. At the end of the day, it doesn't matter how efficient a nanny you have: if that child is not well, it has to take preference over your job.

You can't manage both. . . . Once you make a commitment to a company you have a big responsibility and it doesn't stop there. ... Most of the staff here are men with wives, families, mortgages and school fees to pay. You've got to take it all pretty seriously. It has to be a total commitment."

Beverly Anderson, a single parent, believes that women are locked into a set of choices that don't affect men.

"If you choose to have babies you become responsible for another human being, but the way things are arranged at the moment, it is *women* who have to accept the responsibility. Culture, not biology, is forcing young girls to say: 'Take yourself seriously, be independent, earn money' or : 'Have babies'.

I spend quite a lot of my time talking to sixth-formers about sexual equality. What I try to say to young girls and boys is: 'This is a problem for *all* of us. Sexual relationships are good and right. The urge to have children is a powerful one, but it has consequences which we have not sorted out.' It's important, I feel, for girls to have a settled, trained skill before babies, for everybody's sake.

We need to make men accept their responsibility for child

rearing, because unless we can do that, women are continually going to be lumbered with a dual burden – and that is the crux of the matter.

A lot of women let men off yet again by buying other women to help, and that way they just conceal the problem.

> *'We need to make men accept their responsibility for child rearing, because unless we can do that, women are continually going to be lumbered with a dual burden . . .'*

Women are faced either with being wicked in that they neglect their children, or with buying another woman as a substitute. That doesn't seem to me to have moved us very far forward at all. The problem we still need to confront is the role of men."

Linda Agran claims not to know one successful woman in *her* line of business who is married with children, a situation which she feels has a lot to do with timing and the pressures of the biological clock. Just at the point when a woman might be getting her first real career break – say, early thirties – she might also be contemplating being a mother. It's 'Is my future in this company really looking good?' versus 'Should I have a child? And if I have a child, will I be able to return to a career at the same level?'

"Many women are dissuaded, and they are quite right to be. . . . No *man* has to say: 'I don't know whether I should do this job because I'm thinking of having a baby.' . . ."

Why, asks Agran, should women feel they have to combine the two? "I think the mistake is to attempt it. That's the wrong path. The path is to get society to change and to get men to relinquish some of the power they have, and to understand that there has to be a *flexibility*. . . .

I don't see why women have to be whizzes in the kitchen, at the ironing, rearing children and listening to their garbage all day long, *and* have a career. Stuff that!

In America, you can take up to five years off work and return to your previous position with your future opportunities unspoiled. I think that is exactly what should happen here: women should be entitled to leave, have their children, get them past the puking stage and return with their opportunities guaranteed.

We should also have flexible hours whereby a woman can come in and work as and when it suits her. This is not hard to organize. It's always been cited as terribly difficult because of *security*. . . . There is always an excuse for not doing something and I'm tired that, in the eighties, so little has been achieved."

An an enthusiastic mother, **Beverly Anderson** feels passionately about the unfair choices imposed on women by the way that society is structured to suit men.

"It seems to me wasteful of society to force a woman to choose between being an honourable parent and an efficient worker. Men earn their living in a way which denies their parenthood, and that forces on to women a huge burden which is not a fair, or even sensible, one. It denies society *their* skills and competence, and the only answer is for men to take up their share of domestic responsibilities, enabling women to use their skills in the marketplace.

Everybody will benefit from that, but at present men have no incentive to acquire these new skills. Furthermore, child-rearing and domestic organization have no status and power, and that makes it doubly difficult to persuade them to do their share.

The system is geared to partnered men, who arrive at nine o'clock in their clean shirts and go home in the evening to a hot meal prepared by their wives.

I've sat around committee tables with men at 10 a.m. and by that time I feel as if I've already done a full day's work. I've got my son to school, remembered the dinner money, made a medical appointment. . . . I have organized two lives, and these guys slip into their seats in their nice clean shirts and they are free to stay out till seven at night wheeling and dealing. . . . I work twice as hard as they do, but because they have the time in which to make it clear they are competent, they will always be taken, professionally, more seriously than me. I feel, not just for myself but for women as a group, that this is an outrageous misallocation – and it's got to stop!"

Linda Agran agrees: "We in this country are losing out so much in terms of input. We are losing some of the best people, because they are actively discouraged. . . . I believe the only way out of the trouble is through positive discrimination and it's got to come from the top down."

'I work twice as hard as they do, but because they have the time in which it makes it clear they are competent, they will always be taken, professionally, more seriously than me.'

Apart from the 'ludicrous' hours, adds **Agran**, another drawback for women is the fact that much of the important contact between managers happens at the end of the day's work, and the moment a woman says: 'I've got to go', it's : 'Well, there you are, you see?'

"Very often these discussions are held in places where women can't go anyway. I have three writers working for me who are members of the Garrick club. I can't meet them at the Garrick because they don't allow women to become members. It is unacceptable. . . ."

Women are learning valuable lessons from this male 'ghetto' situation and have begun to set up their own networks as a source of mutual support and contact. In traditionally male-dominated preserves like the railway industry, they can be a lifeline.

While working as traffic manager at Willesden Junction station in London, **Sarah Kendall** helped develop an informal support network of women, including trainee signalwomen and guards.

"What has kept me going is being in touch with other women and getting support from them, because as a woman in this industry you can feel very isolated."

Her social life is curtailed by the nature and hours of the job. "I have a very supportive set of friends who have put up with a lot over the years."

Carol Wilson, Former head of A and R, Polydor, is in the sort of profession where work and leisure activities frequently overlap. "I have a furious social life. Most of it takes place in the West End. I might have dinner with someone at Groucho's before a gig.

I like to be in bed by midnight, but I do go out most nights and out to lunch most days. I try to quieten it down at weekends."

Socially, women in high profile professions may have to cope with the fears and insecurities of their male partners. If you are seen as successful in your work, this can alter the balance of power in your sexual relationships. The mere fact that *you* hold the purse-strings, the higher salary which is the passport to expense account lunches or a wild night out on the town, makes you very much the upfront, dominant partner.

Linda Agran: "When my bloke and I go to a restaurant for dinner and he's taking *me*, *I* book the table (because if it's in my name we get a decent table), I get the wine list and I get the bill! A lot of men find this very threatening, but he finds it quite amusing, bless his heart."

She is right. A lot of men find it hard to come to terms with a woman partner who is a high achiever.

Often, it is less the financial inequality than the amount of time spent on work that can cause friction with partners.

Linda Agran: "Fifteen or twenty years ago I was involved with guys who did find it a bone of contention and got jealous and fed up with the whole thing. Now, my work is so much part of me that my bloke is actually quite proud of me. . . . And that's another thing: men often change tack. First, they like the idea of you having a career, and then it's – 'But where's my dinner?' I've never ironed a shirt in my life and I'm not going to start now. I'm happy to employ other people to do it, and that's great. . . . Any time that I'm not spending working, or with the people I love, I'll be sleeping, but I ain't gonna be ironing!

A lot of the work that women are perceived as having to do is a waste of time. It is a constant treadmill. . . . I like the idea of hitting peaks, achieving something, wrapping it up, finishing with it, then doing something else. That's why gardening and housework don't appeal to me ... I mean, I want it spotless but I'm not going to do it!

I see my job as a way of life. Most of my friends are involved in the same business. I work seven days a week. I read scripts and see people at weekends, and I love to give dinner parties. The problem is the shopping ... It's a case of whizzing around Sainsbury's at nine in the morning because we've got a 9.30 meeting. I need a *wife*, that's what I need!"

Vivien Padwick employs a full-time housekeeper. "My social life is there to *enjoy*, not do more work. . . ."

She doesn't worry about men feeling threatened or diminished by her wealth and high profile existence. "I've probably been out with more millionaires than anybody I know!", she remarks, adding that she has been out with the other sort, too.

"A couple of relationships have failed where the male hasn't any money. It might be all right if they are nice, intelligent males and you can say 'Look , I'm ever so lucky. I've come into some money and want somebody to enjoy it with'. I had a boyfriend like that for eighteen months . . . Someone offered me two million pounds to buy the company and I turned it down because I was going out with him and I thought I would never know whether he wanted the money or me.

Every man I ever meet says the same thing to me: 'I imagine it's difficult for you to get boyfriends because most other men just couldn't live with somebody in your position', but *they* always claim to be the exception to the rule!"

— '*A*nother drawback for women is the fact that much of the important contact between managers happens at the end of the day's work, and the moment a woman says: "I've got to go", it's: "Well, there you are, you see?" ' —

Like Wadlow, Padwick and Agran enjoy the freedom of living alone. Padwick, when she started her career, never thought she'd be sitting there 20-odd years later, unmarried. She has never deliberately *chosen* not to have children but believes that "the first ten years of a child's life are much more important than a high-powered job."

Linda Agran says she has never really lived with anyone

"and I don't want to know what kind of a day they've had. Selfish is a word that is used, and it's considered to be a Bad Thing. Selfish means putting yourself first. So, what I would rather do is come home pissed as a pudding, in a furious temper or whatever and, if I want to, get undressed and go straight under the duvet and not talk to a soul, or sit in front of the TV eating beans out of a tin. I need that *time* and then I'm a reasonably normal human being for when he *is* around.

Too many women walk through the door apologizing. I know more women who walk in the door yelling 'Sorry I'm late'. . . . They've all done it. Most of them are now divorced."

Beverly Anderson has found that her natural assertiveness in business has impinged on her relationships with men.

"I have been unsuccessful in a lot of my relationships because I think men find it confusing. . . . I'm quite diffident personally, and unassertive in my relationships with men. I was brought up in the business world but also brought up to be very deferential to men, and the trouble is that this is a contradictory way of behaving. I understand why it happens, but I'm no more competent at dealing with men than any other woman. What happens is that they confuse competence with self-sufficiency, and so there has been a personal disadvantage in my being forthright, especially in British culture."

The real test of a relationship comes when, like area manager **Sarah Kendall**, you are offered a plum post in a totally different area. It might be the opposite end of the country and would entail a fair old upheaval for both of you. Whose job, whose future, comes first? His move – or yours?

Sarah Kendall accepted the post at Carlisle only when she was certain that her journalist boyfriend would move up there with her. "His support is essential, and the support of other friends. Most of my friends and family are London-based." Her colleagues at Carlisle were mostly her parents' age and she found they had little in common."

Your partner's feelings about moving depend, of course, on the kind of job he is in, how thrustingly ambitious he is, and whether he is prepared to compromise – to forego *his* career prospects for yours. Will he mind being upstaged as well as uprooted?

When invited to give a talk at the 1986 Institute of Directors conference, executive search consultant Hilary Sears rang several of her competitors and asked them: "Have you ever placed a woman?" They gave two main reasons why they had not done so: the difficulty of finding women at the right level (the £30,000 a year mark), and the fact that women would be less open to the idea of moving than men would be, because they value security and maybe lack confidence to switch to another company.

> ‘*Ian needs to have a flexible attitude towards mobility, otherwise I couldn't pursue my career to its full extent and would have to turn opportunities down. So he will have to "up sticks" and go with me.*’

"We see a future with one company, and think that if we are loyal that company will promote us," Sears says.

This could mean a move *internally* – to another branch or area: standard procedure, for instance, in banks and building societies.

When you and your partner first got together, you must have discussed the possibility of your promotion and what this would imply for both of you. Convention decrees that, in most cases, a woman follows her husband, nurturing his career as well as their children. Whither the job goes, she is expected to accompany him. It's an area that is changing, albeit slowly, and the whole question of whose career has priority needs to be reassessed in each individual case.

Some couples compromise by living separately during the week and getting together at the weekends. But how many people these days (apart from MPs) are in a position to run two full-time homes, perhaps hundreds of miles apart, and with all the expense and logistics of commuting that this would entail?

> '*The opportunities are there if you can meet the society's criteria. If you have the ability, get professionally qualified and are willing to move around the country, you will definitely get promoted. Unfortunately, a lot of women are not prepared to move, because their husband's job has to come first.*'

One woman who put her career cards on the table right from the start is Jane Bradley, Manager, Manpower Research at the Halifax Building Society's head office. Building society job grades run from one (basic clerk level) to fifteen (senior branch manager). Jane is currently at grade 11 and one of 35 female managers out of the society's total of 753 (figures released in January 1987). She started out as a clerk in the Sheffield branch.

Her journey up the managerial ladder has involved several moves to different areas of the country, including Hull (departmental manager), Leeds (personnel administration – assistant personnel manager) and finally, to Head Office (in September 1986) and her present job in personnel. (Manpower Research is a newly created wing of the Manpower Planning Department.)

More moves are highly likely as future opportunities come her way. Her husband, Ian, is a screenprinter. They agreed before getting married that they would forego having a family. Children simply didn't enter into Jane's scheme of things.

They discussed careers and agreed that Jane's should come first, as her promotion and financial prospects were far greater than Ian's. She wants very much to get to the top. She is just 30.

"Ian needs to have a flexible attitude towards mobility, otherwise I couldn't pursue my career to its full extent and would have to turn opportunities down. So he will have to 'up sticks' and go with me.

I don't think he would like the idea very much, but I've told him the position and he knows the score."

They never talk about work. Neither knows or understands much about the other's job.

For Jane, the hardest part is trying to maintain a healthy balance between the demands of the office and her social life. There has also been the long slog of examinations, with study having to be slotted into leisure time.

"The opportunities are there if you can meet the society's criteria. If you have the ability, get professionally qualified and are willing to move around the country, you will definitely get promoted. Unfortunately, a lot of women are not prepared to move, because their husband's job has to come first."

Outside influences – husband, family, friends – 'impose on' women and hold them back. But Jane is not an advocate of positive discrimination. "You can't bend the rules just to create openings for women. I have always felt this building society to be fair and equal, but you must be willing to play by the rules."

With or without family ties, your social life will have to submit to your working life. Friends, lovers, husbands, all have to learn to adapt to unsocial hours and sudden changes of plan. They mustn't mind playing second fiddle and should understand that, nine times out of ten, your loyalty to the job overrides your loyalty to them.

Such a situation is only too familiar to women whose husbands are married to their work. The late afternoon phone call to say he has been delayed at the office is more likely to signify a clannish rendezvous in the local pub or club at six pm. In male terms, efficiency is often measured in the number of hours being *seen* to be in the vicinity of the workplace.

Too many companies expect their managers to be on site until seven or eight in the evening, thinks **Linda Stoker**. The long hours combined with pressures of commuting can ruin marriages.

"There is so much divorce in the City, so much stress. . . . Women look at life more holistically. They want to organize their work to fit in with their lives, but they are criticized because of that. They are not in the network that is going down the pub, but they are getting the job done. Men are spinning their jobs out so that they can go to the pub.

One of my theories about men is that most of them need a Wendy House to play in, to escape from their families, the kids. . . . Some men have boats or sheds, others have offices. Staying in the office up in Town is an escape."

6

How To Keep Your Head

---◆---

AND YOUR HEALTH

---◆---

I f you are not careful, the pressure of balancing home and work commitments can take its toll on your health and relationships. Exhaustion can set in as you grapple with two or more sets of priorities. It's all part of the Superwoman syndrome. As women, we inherit a long line of guilt, from our mothers and grandmothers. We long to be the perfect mother/wife/employee/boss. Nothing less will measure up to the exacting standards we set ourselves, and so we drive ourselves until we drop. Not surprisingly, in trying to maintain this delicate balancing act, signs of stress begin to show. We feel edgy, start shouting at the kids and, though each of us would be probably the last to admit it, we feel beleaguered and unable to cope.

Our feelings of stress are frequently caused by the gap between our high expectations and the practical, daily reality of trying to achieve the impossible. Rather than face up to the possibility of failure, we carry on like blind lemmings, caught up in the maelstrom of events. It is almost a form of arrogance. Superwoman must at all times be seen to be managing.

What we should be doing is taking time to quietly reassess the direction of our lives. Instead, we push ourselves even harder, becoming more and more anxious and irritable in the process, kidding ourselves that everything in the home and workplace is running on oiled wheels.

Dr William Mitchell, a clinical psychologist, counsels people suffering from stress. He believes that women are more susceptible than men to the pressures of a business career. "To be a successful female manager you have to be an extraordinary person, and usually much more able than your male counterparts.

> *'What we do to relax is just to go home. You get home and there are two small children rampaging around the place – little people demanding your attention.'*

The trouble is that women like this are not happy with second best in any area of their lives. They come home and think they must produce excellent meals in an immaculate house and be perfect entertainers of their guests.

It is important to control this tendency to demand perfection in all areas. High standards can be obsessional."[27]

He encourages his female patients to try to find interests outside home and work – but when? Squeezing in extra minutes for other things can be a feat of the imagination.

What you need most of all, and what – especially if you are a family woman – is in painfully short supply, is *space*: mental and physical. Any mother knows how emotionally draining small children can be. A survey by *Good Housekeeping* magazine in April 1987 found that looking after children was the greatest source of stress (among 81 per cent of two thousand polled).

The survey showed that the pressures on working women were as dangerous as those on men and that, unless they took account of the warning signs, they would soon suffer the same rates of heart disease as men.

For the woman executive who can afford first-class child care facilities, the problem is perhaps less acute. Some women find this home-centred part of their lives to be an emotional safety valve. Such a complete contrast to the work environment helps to keep any work-related worries in perspective and, in some cases, probably helps to stave off the Superwoman syndrome.

Fashion designer **Betty Jackson** works with her French husband and partner, David, "What we do to relax is just to go home. You can have had the most awful day at work with something going terribly wrong. You get home and there are two small children rampaging around the place – little people demanding your attention and delighted to see you . . . and we do regard our time with them as being quite precious."

Interestingly, single or divorced women came off worse in the *GH* survey than married women. In my own research, however, no woman, irrespective of marital status, seemed immune to the Superwoman trap.

Haematologist **Sally Davies** is widowed and has no children. "I know that I push myself. I want to be first-class at my career. I want to be successful and known throughout the country. I want to be well-dressed and attractive, to have a stunning social life, to run my house efficiently . . . and actually, when you think about what we all want to achieve and drive ourselves to do, no wonder it's terribly tiring. Every so often I say: 'Why am I driving myself this hard?'

I enjoy cooking. I find it therapeutic, creative. It takes up enough time and energy to stop me worrying about other things.

I think this Superwoman syndrome is self-generated by most women. . . . I employ a woman to do all my ironing, cleaning, everything, and once you start paying someone to do all that, I suppose you then move on to using caterers – or you cut a lot of your social life, or you say: 'I will only tread water at work. I'll do my job but I won't develop it or do any committee work'.

I'm a lifeaholic, not a workaholic. I think there's a distinct difference – and that's one reason why I chose haematology. The career structure, though competitive, is not too long and the hours not too horrendous. I wanted a job that was compatible with an active life."

Barbara Switzer (Deputy General Secretary of TASS, the manufacturing union) is married, with no children. Her husband, Michael, is an active member of TASS. She regards her life as 'extremely stressful'. She works long hours (leaving home at 7.30 am and rarely returning before 8 pm). The 25-mile journey from her home north of Watford to the TASS offices in Wandsworth, South London, can take up to an hour and a half. "It's taught me to be a calm driver! I can't afford to get aggravated or I'd feel as if I'd done a day's work before I got there. . . .

You have to be tough and fit. Sometimes I feel I'm going mad, and it's 'Why am I doing this?' but you just have to get on with it. You have to remove as many of the other areas of stress in your life as you can and try to live as normal a life as possible. . . .

I do lose sleep over work and find it difficult to switch off, especially when important things are going on, like conferences, because you have to be on the ball all the time. The pressure comes on and you have to put in the extra effort. . . .

That's what makes the few weekends off very precious – and holidays. We go boating down the Thames once a year for a week. Most of the time, when I'm away from work, I just want to put my feet up. In the summer months I relax in the garden when I can. I like to listen to traditional jazz. I like having people at home, sitting around chatting. Your home becomes very valuable to you when you don't see it very often."

Katharine Whitehorn escapes whenever she can to the family's 20-foot motor cruiser on the river Thames. "One of the best kinds of holidays we ever have," she says, "is where we simply shift the whole circus to somewhere hotter and Gavin works and I don't."

Jean Wadlow never takes proper holidays, and hasn't had one since she started the company. "I take four of five long weekends a year and do something really super like go to the South of France, or a castle in Scotland. That's what I enjoy and I come back totally refreshed."

She claims to be a stranger to stress. "I don't think you could be in this business if you got uptight about things. Obviously, I have bad days but I don't think 'Oh my God, I've got to relax'.

> *Your home becomes very valuable to you when you don't see it very often.*

I like Saturday mornings. I'll get up about seven, get the newspaper, go back to bed with my breakfast tray and rarely leave the house before ten if I can avoid it. It is the time when my friends call me and when I make all my personal telephone calls, so that's my relaxation.

Work is my hobby and my hobbies are related to my work: the cinema, theatre, opera and music."

Bank manager **Betty Guyatt** reads and rides. She is a member of the Civil Service Riding Club and does aerobics twice a week: "It works off a lot of worry . . . and it helps *perspective*."

Yoga helps **Carol Wilson** to keep stress at bay. "I have practised about forty minutes of Iyenga yoga every day for more than ten years. It sorts out the mind – and body. You have to concentrate hard on the balance. It's a bit like skiing: very physical, gruelling ... I usually ski every year. I find active things more relaxing than sitting around.

An Iyenga class leaves you bursting with energy. It's wonderful. I can get up in the morning aching all over, feel sick, can't think straight and all I want to do is turn over and go back to sleep, but I crawl out of bed and do my forty minutes yoga, and by the end of that time I feel normal again. Sometimes I'll do it at the end of the day as well."

Theatre director **Susan Todd** practises meditation. She also enjoys gardening and going to the gym. But on the whole, she would much prefer to be working. "When one has time off in the theatre, it's because one is unemployed or hasn't got enough work, and so one is worrying about money. I find it hard, when I'm unemployed, to use that time well. I think: 'I'll do some serious reading and do all those things which I've meant to do' – and I don't."

Actress **Josette Simon** has learned to play the saxophone – "purely for my own enjoyment". She practises regularly and finds it a wonderful relaxation and a good way of combating stress. "Anything can happen in this business. It's so precarious. I don't take anything for granted. Most actresses I know are plagued with self-doubt and insecurity. That never goes away from you.

I am not very good at being out of work. After a while comes the feeling you might never work again. You need a lot of self-belief and a thick, thick skin."

Each woman who talked to me has her own way of handling stress. Some (for example, Jean Wadlow) are scarcely aware of it, while for others stress is almost part of their staple diet and they cannot function without a high dose of it.

Some have neither time nor inclination for outside interests. Others somehow manage to organize theatre visits or dinner parties at the end of a taxing working day.

As Rosemary Burr sees it: "Most successful women thrive on a high degree of activity and their stress tolerance is probably way above the average. They tend to live their lives at relatively full throttle."[28]

Temperament and physiology come into the picture, too. There are the vagaries of the menstrual cycle to consider. If you suffer from pre-menstrual tension (PMT), you should try wherever possible to plan ahead so that your workload is not

— '*Most successful women thrive on a high degree of activity and their stress tolerance is probably way above the average.*' —

too heavy during the week before your period. The problems of PMT have been well documented, as have the remedies (vitamin B6 in moderate doses for about ten days beforehand is one of the best energizers I know) and I don't intend to go into this subject here.

All I would say is: be aware of your personal mood swings, but don't be defeated by them, and try to avoid too many commitments immediately before your period begins. At the same time, don't use PMT as an excuse for poor work performance. It's sometimes tempting, when a mistake or misunderstanding occurs, to put it down to the time of the month. If you really want to be accepted on equal terms with men, you must be prepared to compete on equal terms – and if that means coming to work with a splitting head, sore boobs and aching legs, then so be it.

If you allow your hormones to rule you, then the weaker sex tag will stick. Don't give men any more ammunition against you or other women. Don't give them the opportunity to say: 'We had a woman and look what happened. . . . ' Put a foot wrong and they will stamp on it.

Remember: you have a responsibility to the other women coming after you. You could be their future role model. I am not suggesting for a moment that you should shut down your emotions as men have been taught to do for generations past. But you must learn to control them. There are times when it is

> *'For working women, most of the stress arises from conflict about priorities. You have to develop a gut knowledge of what is important . . . '*

in your interest to hide or modify your feelings, so as not to feed male prejudice about women's competence.

If you feel out of joint because someone has upset you – questioned your judgement or criticized a decision you have made in good faith – make for the ladies' cloakroom at the earliest opportunity. It's often the only place where you can be sure of any peace or personal space. Practise breathing deeply and, if it makes you feel better, have a good weep. Let out your feelings and then carry on as normal.

There probably isn't much time to really let go, so when you get home that evening, have a long hot bath and an early night. Talk to a close friend if you can.

Ann Burdus: "I have a feeling that if women suffer from stress in their jobs – and I do, like anyone else – it's because we mainly do what we are doing as a challenge to ourselves, and when we don't live up to our own expectations (or think we might let ourselves down), that's when we suffer from stress. It's almost self-induced. . . . Being busy is not stressful. Worrying about it is."

Dr June Huntingdon, of the King's Fund College in London advises senior nurses and health service administrators on how to avoid stress, and she has devised a number of techniques to help women. "For working women, most of the stress arises from conflict about priorities. You have to develop a gut knowledge of what is important. Otherwise, you will suffer internal conflict, and when you can't manage yourself you will certainly not be able to manage other people.

We have to accept that we can't achieve 150 per cent standards in all areas of our lives. So we have to choose which parts are important."[29]

In-house counselling services can provide a valuable safety net. As one company manager said, "The benefits in moral and mental terms are so apparent. We don't have to justify it financially."

In the long run, you will alleviate stress symptoms by leading a healthier lifestyle – by making sure you have a sensible, balanced diet and plenty of *regular* exercise. It's an established medical fact that vigorous exercise three or more times a week helps to stave off depression and tension.

It also helps you relax, improves your circulation and protects against heart disease. Not least, it gives you greater energy, an essential commodity for all high-achieving women.

Just as personal ambition is about stretching your mental powers, physical fitness is about stretching your body so that it attains peak condition and flexes your mind in the process. As the erstwhile Health Education Council put it, "The purpose of fitness is to add more life to years, not just years to life."

You needn't go as far as some British companies whose employees have been letting out their frustrations in war-gaming activities. According to Russell Powell, who helped set up War Games in a twelve-acre wood near Ormskirk with a partner, Simon Brookes, the chance to zap squashy airgun pellets full of yellow dye at the managing director is the perfect way to get rid of stress and aggression. One executive said his company regarded war-gaming as a valid means of getting management and workforce together.

It's not an all-male pursuit, either. Women, apparently, take about a fifth of the places in the day-long sessions. "There is no actual fighting, so they are on a par with the men – and some of them can run faster", said Brookes.[30] Well, that's a relief, though it may not do much for your promotion prospects. . . .

The best activities for stamina make you slightly out of breath and keep you moving for twenty minutes or more. This type of exercise is aerobic and, apart from actual aerobics, it can include jogging, cycling, swimming.

Find the kind of exercise that suits you – and enjoy it. Treat it as a pleasure, not a punishment. Take it at your own pace. Start slowly, gradually building up your strength so that you don't overtax flabby or under-used muscles. Warm up first with bends and stretches, and cool down afterwards by walking slowly for a few minutes. Don't exercise until it hurts.

> *'If you really want to be accepted on equal terms with men, you must be prepared to compete on equal terms – and if that means coming to work with a splitting head, sore boobs and aching legs, then so be it.'*

It's easy to keep saying: 'I haven't the time'. You really should *make* time for keeping fit, especially if you are in a sedentary occupation. You owe it to yourself to get into the habit of exercising regularly. A few minutes a day is far more effective, and safer, than a one-off session a week. Set aside a definite time each day and stick to it, a time that fits into your work routine – but avoiding the hour or so after mealtimes.

You will be surprised how much fitter you start to feel. Not only will you toughen up muscles you never knew were there, but your skin will glow and your head will feel a lot clearer. The spin-off from all this will be greater efficiency and a more positive attitude to life in general which will spill over into your work, improving your ability to make decisions and cope with crises as and when they occur. It's the holistic approach where mind influences body and vice versa.

Yoga and meditation are perhaps the best examples of this mind/body interaction, though simple relaxation techniques can achieve similar results. By learning to control your breathing and posture, you learn to relax and experience a wonderful sense of wellbeing.

If you are over 35 and have had poor health or are in any doubt about what form of exercise is best for you, do see your doctor. If you are fairly unfit, brisk walking is a good way to start an exercise regime. Try using the stairs instead of the lift. I personally find this no hardship because of a lifelong phobia of lifts. I will cheerfully walk up ten flights of stairs rather than endure being confined cheek by jowl with strangers in a flimsy moving box. How so many able-bodied people can be per-suaded to use this horrendous form of transport, sometimes travelling no further than the mezzanine floor, is beyond my understanding. Is it habit? The herd instinct? Sheer laziness? Or Mass Masochism?

A word or two on smoking. Despite all the dire warnings about dangers to health, evidence points to an increasing number of women turning to cigarettes. It's not hard to see why they are beginning to outnumber male smokers. A woman in an executive or managerial position has generally had to struggle long and hard to get where she is – and to consolidate that position. Her performance is often more closely scrutinized than that of a man at the equivalent grade or level. In addition, she may be faced with the eternal, exhausting battle between work and family.

However, all the good intentions in the world about personal fitness won't mean a light unless a genuine effort is made to give up smoking. Apart from all the other risks that have been cited (and passive smoking is one of them), smoking reduces your ability to take vigorous exercise. Unless you stop, you won't reap much benefit from any exercise regime.

We are all becoming more stress-conscious, especially those of us who work in inner-city areas. Now, there's a new phenomenon called 'Big Bang' stress which, we are told, can lead to burn-out and even total physical collapse. City Health Care are teaching executives how to forestall it. They run a health-screening programme which at present monitors seven times as many men as women. However, according to director Malcolm Emery, "those women we see have often encountered extra pressures in their drive to reach the top. . . . Women also suffer because they don't have the traditional watering holes to retreat to and relax after a long day."[31]

As well as a full medical assessment (including mammograph and cervical smear), doctors proffer techniques on stress management – such as taking a more relaxed attitude to work, and learning to delegate.

One place that has long since come to mean a mecca of peace for women and men who work in the City of London, is the Guild Church of St Mary Woolnoth. For more than a decade, lunchtime classes in relaxation have been held at the church. Balm to their souls – and surely an excellent blueprint for other urban areas?

We all need a break from routine, even the most diehard workaholics. Sometimes a weekend in a country inn is sufficient to revive tired brain cells. Pottering about at home can be therapeutic if you are normally there so seldom that you've forgotten what colour the sitting room walls are. But it can be counter-productive as you might well discover numerous jobs that need doing, in which case it will hardly be a rest cure. Compulsive decorators, take note.

If you run your own business, it is essential to get right away from the tyranny of the telephone. However, many self-employed women I know are loath to take holidays. It's down to a mixture of guilt (the work ethic dies hard) and curiosity about what they might be missing if they venture too far for too long. More than a week and they start to get itchy feet.

It is important to choose the right kind of holiday for *you*. All too often, holidays can generate their own peculiar tensions.

Professor Cary Cooper, one of Britain's leading stress experts, believes that family holidays can be anything but relaxing for the woman concerned. "With dual career couples

> *'Some people are completely unsuited to the traditional two-week break. Type A's, who are ambitious and aggressive, will be hysterical because it can take them that long to unwind.'*

it's still the woman who bears the brunt of domestic duties, so when she goes on holiday she tends to say she's off-duty and the man has to shoulder a greater share. That puts a strain on the marriage. Some people are completely unsuited to the traditional two-week break. Type A's, who are ambitious and aggressive, will be hysterical because it can take them that long to unwind."[32]

According to a survey by scientists at Cambridge University's clinical school in 1987, greater sexual equality has resulted in more Type A women: ambitious, forceful, high-achieving. There are now as many Type A women as men.

The survey, funded by the tobacco industry and featuring the health and lifestyle of more than nine thousand people, revealed a sizeable health gap between North and South, reflecting the social inequalities of these two regions.

It also revealed a further health gap – between women and men. Women were found to report higher rates of illness than men at all ages. And instances of high blood pressure are almost as high among women as men. They are prescribed more drugs than men are, although they enjoy a healthier diet: more wholefoods, fruit and salads, and less fried food.

The survey stressed that people who take exercise think more quickly and have faster reaction times than those who lead sedentary lives.

The majority of my interviewees gave tenacity and determination as the most important requirements for success, and the exercise habit certainly reinforces these attributes.

> *Women do not like to complain because it means they have to stand out and challenge what is often considered "normal" behaviour.*

There is one source of stress that is not self-inflicted, and that is sexual harassment. Sedley and Benn define it as "repeated, unreciprocated and unwelcome comments, looks, jokes, suggestions or physical contact that might threaten a woman's job security or create a stressful or intimidating working environment. Physical contact can range from touching to pinching, through to rape."[33]

Sexual harassment, they say, is "one of the most insidious

ways in which men unconsciously impose and reinforce their power."[34]

Agony columnist Anna Raeburn goes so far as to describe *all* sexual harassment as a form of rape. It is "one of the ways in which men keep women down. They view us solely as the adjuncts of men and therefore as common property."[35]

If you work in an office, whatever your level of seniority, chances are that you will at some stage have had to fend off the wandering hands of a male colleague. And if you decline to 'co-operate'or become upset by the approach, you are likely to be considered prudish, offhand or a bad sport.

As one woman I know, once a secretary, now a lawyer, puts it: "A woman in an office with men is very open to feelings of inadequacy and manipulation. She has to appear attractive, and the more attractive she is the more she gets put down. You just can't win."

When I was Women's Editor on a group of regional newspapers in South East London, casual clothes were the norm and I regularly turned up to the office in trousers. On the one day in the year that I had been booked to speak at a women's luncheon, I decided to slip on a dress, whereupon my fellow reporters greeted me with a loud whooping chorus of – 'Ooh, look! She's got legs!'

Leers and gibes from the linotype operators downstairs were a regular occurrence which I learned to ignore, much as I learned to ignore the galaxy of tits and bums which adorned the walls of the Print Room. I affected a kind of nonchalant, gum-chewing, freewheeling air as I floated through the fog of smoke and four-letter words to check on the progress of my women's feature pages.

Though galling at the time, such incidents are relatively minor ones. Fear of being isolated or ostracized makes us laugh along with our male colleagues at our own expense, rather than risk being thought huffy or humourless.

Such incidents, we tell ourselves, are mere occupational hazards, to be tolerated with good grace and gritted teeth, a bit of harmless frivolity and fun.

Sexual harassment is not a new phenomenon, but it is only in recent years that women have begun to organize around the issue. It has only just begun to come out of the closet. "Just as domestic violence has been accepted as normal within a marital relationship – women being considered the property of their husbands – so sexual harassment has been considered normal behaviour in the relationship between men and women at work throughout history." [36]

If it has happened to you, you may have been too scared or embarrassed to stick your neck out and protest. We are, after all, in a recession and jobs are short. "Women also do not like to complain because it means they have to stand out and challenge what is often considered 'normal' behaviour. It is probably very threatening for men to have their behaviour looked at in this way and they react by trivializing the matter and undermining the women complainants. [37]

You may even have felt that whatever happened was somehow *your* fault and that you had somehow invited the unwanted attention.

Sexual harassment is notoriously hard to prove. It mirrors, and is part of, our sexist society, but is more direct and personal than *sexism*, and, therefore, more distressing to the woman concerned. "There is a very fine line between harassment and discrimination; indeed, the former may in the end be easier to fight than the social prejudices and assumptions of a conservative management." [38]

Former Manpower Services Commission Chairman Bryan Nicholson is aware of the problem, but seems to think that women themselves are partly to blame. "The persistent failure of women to reach higher levels of management is only one manifestation of a problem that exists throughout the world of work. That problem is male prejudice, and it shows itself in many ways, from the pat on the bottom to the girlie calendar on the wall and the sexist remarks. Women have grown so used to such things that they have become part of working life, but while ever they put up with them, true equality will always be over the horizon." [39]

Well, there is strong evidence that women are beginning to fight back and are no longer prepared to suffer in silence the slings and taunts of male chauvinists. To date, most surveys on sexual harassment have been carried out in the United States, thanks to the efforts of the women's movement there. American women have been campaigning against it since the early seventies. A woman had developed a crippling psychosomatic pain in response to sexual harassment at work. Her story sparked off a lengthy investigation by two feminists at Cornell University. A letter which they sent to 300 women's organizations in the United States asking for case studies and other information, led to a well-attended 'speak out' on sexual harassment, the first time the subject had been aired openly.

> *That problem is male prejudice, and it shows itself in many ways, from the pat on the bottom to the girlie calendar on the wall and the sexist remarks.*

Since then, women's organizations such as NOW (the National Organization of Women) have provided legal and counselling advice.

In Britain, the union which has been most active in campaigning against sexual harassment is NALGO, the local government union, which describes the problem as "a threat to a woman's right to a healthy and safe working environment."

Women's officer, Tess Woodcraft: "One of the problems,

we find, is that it is often not that a woman goes and complains about sexual harassment. It is that her work falls off because she starts going sick and thus avoiding the person who is harassing her. Complaints are made about her work and then she has to admit what the real reason is. That immediately casts doubt on what she is saying in a male-dominated world.

Sexual harassment is easy to allege and hard to prove. There is usually nobody else around at the time and it's one person's word against another. It might be regarded as an excuse by the woman to wriggle out of a poor work performance."

In the case of women further up the managerial tree, Woodcraft feels that sexual harassment is used to bring them down a peg or two, "to reaffirm their inferior status. It is therefore used against women seeking to get into public life and management positions, and to remind them they are getting ideas above their station. It is a very powerful weapon against women in that situation. . . .

The nature of sexual harassment means that it can be used against women in a whole range of working situations, in slightly different ways, and when directed against women in management, it reminds them that a woman's role is to be decorative and lightweight."

She cites the example of the social worker whose passionate commitment to one particular case manifests itself in a fiery outburst on the subject to her superior, who tells her: 'You look so attractive when you are angry'.

"Sexual harassment is about power, and the more powerful women become the more threatened men feel. It is either intended to reflect men's power, or to remind a woman that she is not all-powerful."

The health risk can be so great that a woman, after exhibiting stress-related symptoms, may feel compelled to leave her job.

In her book, *The Office Workers' Survival Handbook*, Marianne Craig cites the office boss or manager as a serious work hazard, along with fluorescent strip lighting and copying machine fumes.

Sedley and Benn insist that not only is sexual harassment a health and safety question, it is "inextricably bound up with power relationships in the workplace" and a major facet of discrimination against working women. [40]

Although sexual harassment is probably most common in situations where a man is in a position of authority over a

> *Sexual harassment is about power, and the more powerful women become the more threatened men feel. It is either intended to reflect men's power, or to remind a woman that she is not all-powerful.*

woman, it can – and does – happen to a woman whatever her rank, age, looks or marital status. Any woman can find herself the victim of masculine wiles.

Linda Agran: "I was appointed to a job with a large, well-established film company. I had at this time, I thought, developed a reputation for being quite good at my work. We were shooting a film in Paris, and we flew out there to ensure that the film was going according to the script, which I had approved.

We saw the film and had an argument, because the film was not the film that I had approved. The final scene had been changed.

We came back from the shooting, went out to dinner with the producer, returned to the hotel and he said: 'Let's have a drink and discuss what we're going to do for the meetings tomorrow'. I did that – and he jumped on me.

I said: 'Look, let's just forget about this. I'll go to my room now and we won't mention it again', and he said: 'Why do you think I gave you the job? I could have given it to anybody'. I said: 'Well, you carry on like that and you've got my resignation tomorrow morning'."

Vivien Padwick: "If you've got to barter sex against success, tell them to go to hell. I've come across it occasionally, and it's a question of keeping to your own moral ethics. If you are that nature, or a prostitute, fine. If it doesn't worry someone, good

> **'***If* you've got to barter sex against success, tell them to go to hell. I've come across it occasionally, and it's a question of keeping to your own moral ethics.**'**

luck to them. *I* couldn't do it. The only thing I would say is: 'Get it strictly in writing first!'"

She had her first work-related 'proposition' when she was on *Vogue* magazine. She was in charge of Vogue Travel and travelling the world. At the time of the incident in question, she was in Malta.

How did she handle the situation? "With rage and fury! I told him to get lost. It was this Maltese man, Alfredo. He'd only met me once for about ten minutes in the middle of a meeting and asked if I could come back later that day. I went back and he wasn't available, but he'd left a message that he desperately wanted to see me.

I had the invitation out to dinner, but things got very heavy at two in the morning. . . . I can talk myself out of most things and I did this time, too. I got the contracts. Don't know how I wangled that one! I wanted the business. I knew what was expected of me and I manipulated the situation.

I was staying at one of the best hotels in Malta. I was there three weeks. The service was superb, everyone was so friendly, and about the second or third evening I dressed for dinner in all my finery. It was the most fabulous restaurant, the orchestra was playing and there was me with about 50 waiters, the only guest in the hotel.

The manager, who was German, turned up. It turned out his wife was away for six months, so we were alone. He'd obviously wanted some 'light entertainment'. . . . I was telling him this story about the Maltese man and the trouble I'd had and he then came on like my father, sort of out to protect me. It was all dire jealousy and he wouldn't let any of my business calls come through to me.

When I went out one evening he was standing at the door: 'Where are you going tonight? I insist you cannot go out alone'. Red roses were coming to my room. It was awful.

A few days later an English convention turned up and I started getting friendly with them. The manager wouldn't let me talk to them. He kept on interrupting me and saying: 'We are having dinner tonight'. I was getting so uptight. But all these English people saw what was going on and I had their backing, so I reported him. He got fired."

While researching her book, *Stress and the Woman Manager*, co-author Dr Marilyn Davidson discovered that sexual harassment was very much a hidden issue in the workplace. From the initial mailing of questionnaires she noticed that, on the section reserved for 'any other comments', a large number of women had mentioned instances of sexual harassment (although not all had defined it in those terms).

A survey by the Alfred Marks Bureau in 1982 showed that regular sexual remarks or jokes upset half of all women employees. The survey included specific examples, some relating to managerial jobs: "Two female managers . . . said that their senior managers had made it quite obvious that if they wanted to be upgraded they would have to be 'nice' to him. Other cases of bribes were cited with offers of holidays, preferential treatment and company benefits." . . . "A manager explained to a female member of his staff that her promotion depended on her willingness to accept his sexual advances."

Whatever form it takes, sexual harassment is more about the lust for power than physical lust. Professor Cary Cooper, co-author of *Stress and the Woman Manager*, sees it like this:

"Sometimes it's not what you say, it's the way you say it, or the gestures. It's insidious behaviour that could be construed as a compliment or gallantry. Often the comments occur when men are doing a macho number in front of others, ganging up to put a woman down. They are effectively saying, 'I'm more senior and more valuable in the hierarchy than you are'. It happens most often when they feel threatened by the woman or competing with them for promotion. . . . "[41]

The TUC definition of sexual harassment is, quite simply, 'unwanted verbal or sexual advances'. In a booklet on the subject the Society of Civil and Public Servants warns that offenders could face legal action if they failed to stop harassing co-workers.

Because of complex legal processes and shortage of financial support, this is not an easy option and, as Sedley and Benn put it, should be seen as 'a last resort, not a first option'.[42]

There is no law against sexual harassment as such. Although, under the terms of the Sex Discrimination Act, women can take cases to an industrial tribunal, few cases have been heard in this way, largely because of the difficulty of proving sexual harassment.

One woman, however, has been successful. Elly Walsh was sacked from her job as an executive with a recruiting company after pouring a pint of lager over a male colleague who had been sexually harassing her at work. She also delivered him a brisk smack. Her case, in 1983, was the first to be won at a tribunal under the Sex Discrimination Act (most cases have previously been brought under the section of the law relating to 'unfair dismissal'). Although the company declined to pay her compensation (she was awarded £2,000-plus), the publicity surrounding her case has encouraged other women to take similar action.

One recent movie, *Business As Usual*, features a graphically told story of sexual harassment at work and unfair dismissal. It was written, directed and produced by women, and features actress Glenda Jackson as the central character, Babs. Babs is based on a real-life woman called Audrey who was sacked for defending a colleague (played by Cathy Tyson) who had been sexually harassed at work. A case of Art reflecting Life in a positive way, and a sign that a problem affecting so many women is at last beginning to be taken seriously.

The EOC (Equal Opportunities Commission) is stepping

'*As more women enter organizations, we ought to find out why men are frightened by them and feel the need to devalue them.*'

---

up the fight against sexual harassment. The number of enquiries they have had between 1983 and 1987 has doubled and they claim this is just the tip of the iceberg.

Professor Cary Cooper insists that it is *men's* problem, and suggests that what is needed is not assertiveness training for women but sensitization programmes for men. "As more women enter organizations, we ought to find out *why* men are frightened by them and feel the need to devalue them. We should look at men's negative blockage behaviour in two stages: first with men alone, then in mixed groups.

Men have had years of experience playing organizational politics and learning how to put people down. Unfortunately, women haven't. I think in 20 or 30 years' time, when females are allowed total access to all jobs and are on equal footing with men in pay, status and so on, harassment won't pose such a threat."[43]

He could well be right, but in the meantime the problem won't go away, so what can women do to protect themselves against male colleagues or bosses who won't take 'No' for an answer? The NCCL have recommended certain tactics for dealing with individual situations as and when they arise, and most are given below.

1   Talk to other women at work. Find out if the culprit has behaved in this way before towards any of them.

2   Get together with other women and talk about what to do. Try to form a women's group. If you work in a large organization, you could use a questionnaire to get more information about the experience of other women and their views.

3   Collect evidence of the harassment. Write down what he does or says, and when. Ask a friend or colleague to take note as well. One suggestion from the United States is that women wire themselves up with tape recorders!

4   Ask the harasser to stop behaving in this way. If possible, arrange for a friend or colleague to be with you when you confront him. Be specific about what offends you. Many men are not aware that jokes and touching can be offensive.

5   If you belong to a union, get them to agree to use the established grievance procedure for dealing with cases of sexual harassment as well as other discrimination issues.

6   Put a resolution to your union branch or trades council.

7   Contact your union's equality committee (if there is one) and ask them to take up the issue.

8   Contact the NCCL and/or the EOC for advice.

9   Suggest to senior management that it is in their interests to have a procedure that deals with sexual harassment to improve working conditions.

The Society of Civil and Public Servants, in their pamphlet 'Sexual Harassment – a trade union issue', have included a lengthy section on how to deal with the problem, suggesting various 'negotiating objectives'. In its similarly titled leaflet,

> *Sometimes it's not what you say, it's the way you say it, or the gestures. It's insidious behaviour that could be construed as a compliment or gallantry. Often the comments occur when men are doing a macho number in front of others . . .*

NALGO have specified a six-point plan for pursuing a case of sexual harassment.

In Birmingham, the City Council's women's committee has been running self-defence programmes for its female employees whose work puts them at risk of being attacked or harassed. Women make up two thirds of council staff and have increasingly become victims of violence directed at public sector employees dealing with the casualties of inner city poverty.

Added impetus for the venture came following the death of Birmingham social worker, Frances Betridge, who was battered to death by a client during a domiciliary visit in September 1986. A man has since been gaoled for her murder.

It was back in April 1986 that the Women's Committee

— *'Women should not look down defensively, but engage the Lothario's eye sternly. A low timbre to the voice also works more effectively than a nervous yelp.'* —

recommended, as a priority, measures for dealing with sexual harassment. In November 1986, in a report, 'Council Strategy on Violence Against Women', the Head of the Women's Unit put forward specific recommendations, among them the inclusion of sexual harassment in in-service training, particularly management courses.

Barbara Webster, Head of the Women's Unit: "Women were feeling very unsupported by the management. The attitude appeared to be one where it was not considered all right for women to say 'I feel uncomfortable in this situation'. They felt unable to discuss their fears openly with management."

The unit has since been running seminars for managers to talk about the issues as part of its awareness programme which aims to develop appropriate ways of dealing with aggression in the workplace.

Women managers have seen that it is an issue of concern to them personally. Some have themselves encountered sexual harassment.

It has been suggested that social workers in particular are loath to report attacks or may stay too long in a potentially violent situation for fear of being seen as weak or unprofessional.

Webster and her colleagues agree that sexual harassment in the office is a different proposition altogether. They teach "simple methods of dealing with men who think they have a divine right to stand too close. ... Women should not look down defensively, but engage the Lothario's eye sternly. A low timbre to the voice also works more effectively than a nervous yelp."[44]

The most important thing is not to allow the harassment to drag on before taking action against the perpetrator – for your own peace of mind, long-term health and wellbeing, and also for the sake and safety of other women in the company.

So, if you want to get ahead – and stay ahead – in the marathon of life, look after yourself. Your health and strength are far too precious to be abused or neglected. Personal success or triumph will mean little or nothing without them.

Going It Alone

HOW TO BE AN ENTERPRISING WOMAN

A major spin-off from the high unemployment figures of the eighties is the growth in women entrepreneurs. There are now more than 2.7 million self-employed in Britain, one in ten of the working population. About a quarter of them are women, and between 1981 and 1984 they increased in numbers by 42 per cent.

It takes guts to go it alone. You need an excess of those hallmarks of the successful executive – tenacity and determination – to stay dynamic, sane and solvent.

Yet, for a woman with a saleable idea or product and the enthusiasm to put it across, running her own business can be a more rewarding and less angst-ridden way of achieving personal status than fending off competition within the corporate structure.

Jane Skinner's national women's enterprise development agency, set up in 1986 and based at Aston Management Centre, has opened doors for many aspiring businesswomen. "In the UK women at lower hierarchical levels are frustrated at being unfairly blocked; some choose to start out on their own as the way through this. Such reasons may be particularly strong motivators where the culture and atmosphere of an organization at its senior levels strongly exclude women."[45]

Her agency aims to help unlock women's potential as entrepreneurs by giving them confidence and a positive self-image and, where necessary, providing training and assessment programmes. It advises women on how best to approach banks and prepare a business plan, and also on appropriate dress and behaviour. It also hopes to persuade banks to revise their old-fashioned views of women.

There are plans to set up a 'loan fund of last resort' to help women with a viable business idea but no access to credit.

Skinner hopes her agency will act as a catalyst for a number of locally based women's enterprise agencies. Two pilot projects in the Birmingham area were set up early in 1987 and are aimed at women who might not have previously considered self-employment.

This type of specialist agency has achieved great success in the United States, where women are said to be creating businesses at about five times the rate of men. In 1985, women-owned businesses made up 26 per cent of the total (compared with less than five per cent in 1972).

On the credit side, being your own boss offers:

Flexibility

The opportunity of staggering your hours to fit in with your own needs and lifestyle. More time to spend with the children, the freedom to shop during unsocial hours.

Status

A degree of autonomy which is lacking in most jobs below the top rung of the executive ladder. Unlike most employee roles, you call the tune, you dictate the terms. It's a way of competing with men on truly equal terms, and a means of escape from the shackles of male hierarchies.

Job Fulfilment

The chance to oversee all aspects of the business and, in the case of a private hobby or passion, the additional satisfaction of seeing it put to profitable use.

On the debit side, being your own boss can be fraught with

pitfalls. Before embarking on your project, first ask yourself: 'Can I cope with the highs and lows of self-employment? Will I weather the fluctuations of the market, changeable bank interest rates and so on?'

You many have blossomed as a senior or middle manager but be totally unsuited temperamentally to the 24-hour-a-day commitment of running your own show. What kind of person are you? Are you good at dealing with people? An all-rounder? A risk-taker? Or a born worrier?

Executives and entrepreneurs inhabit two very different worlds and you stand to lose a lot if you fail to do some preliminary homework on *yourself* as well as the type of business you are planning. Forewarned is forearmed.

It's often a help in these situations to compile a kind of balance sheet setting out the pros and cons of your enterprise, simply to clarify it in your own mind.

On the other hand, you don't know till you try! You might be in a dead-end job. You may be feeling frustrated by petty office politics or by an underlying, all-pervasive sexism. This itself can act as a powerful trigger mechanism.

If you have an idea that you are *burning* to sell, all other doubts will fade away or be swept away in your overwhelming enthusiasm. You will forge ahead and nothing in the world will deter you. There is a great deal of truth in the notion that if you want to do something badly enough you will make it in the end.

Having decided that you are true entrepreneurial material, and drawn up your own personal 'balance sheet', what next? Apart from a good (and preferably original) idea or product, you will need, ideally, the following: a sympathetic bank manager who will look kindly, but not patronisingly, on your brainchild; enough initial funding not to give you sleepless nights; a clearly defined marketing strategy; oodles of stamina, unflagging optimism and dedication beyond the call of duty; experience, where possible, in your chosen field.

The first – and, for many women entrepreneurs, *worst* – hurdle is that initial eyeball-to-eyeball meeting with the bank manager. It will almost invariably be a man, a fact which you should take into account when you go to him to present your brilliant new idea. Banks, reflecting the way in which our society is organized, tend to operate on an old-boy basis, and some male bank managers remain locked into a patriarchal timewarp. Women clients, especially if they are young and attractive, are not taken seriously.

Linda Stoker remembers one abortive attempt to sell her training schemes to one of the Big Four banks. "The manager judged me as soon as I walked in the door. He was in his late

> '*What can I do, as a woman, to make it easier for entrepreneurial women to get financial help?*'

fifties, with a public school tie, and he talked to me very pompously.

Everything I suggested he thought of a reason for not doing. He wouldn't budge.

I soon realized that unless I grew some additional parts and went to his school I was wasting my time!"

Betty Guyatt, a branch manager with the Midland Bank in North London, feels that too few aspiring businesswomen receive cash help or encouragement from male managers, even for expansion of established businesses. "This has been expressed to me at various all-women conferences. If a woman has been in business successfully for three or four years and then decides she wants to move to other premises, trying to raise the finance is incredibly difficult."

She asks herself: "What can I do, as a woman, to make it easier for entrepreneurial women to get financial help?" It is this customer relations aspect of the job that most appeals to Ms Guyatt.

"You can be constructive and creative. When a woman comes through the door with a product she wants finance for, and you feel there is a market for this, rather than simply decide to lend the client £5,000 or whatever it takes, you can actually become involved in helping her work out her cash flow, see where her 'break-even' is and say : 'Have you thought of such-and-such a market?'

Even if she has done her homework, there might be areas that you can suggest that she hasn't thought of, so you are working on this thing together in a partnership way."

She believes women tend to be better than men at this sort of personal, co-operative approach. "Giving time and listening is

If a woman has been in business successfully for three or four years and then decides she wants to move to other premises, trying to raise the finance is incredibly difficult.

cost-effective." A growing number of women, particularly black women, are approaching her for financial help to launch their own business ventures. It's a trend she welcomes.

A woman bank manager with Barclays has found that women who come to her requesting funding to start up a small business, are far more *prepared* than men are. "They have thought through the project very methodically and they come into the interview in a far better position to be helped than the average man."

As a client selling your wares, you should use all your powers of persuasion to convince the manager, male or female, that a) you are a Good Risk (not a High Risk), and b) your idea is more than just a sideline. This means having written proof of your intentions in the form of a neatly typed presentation outlining your proposal: its objectives, market, a breakdown of costings, and so on. You need to give full details of your personal circumstances and background (present income, mortgage arrangements, investments) and previous business experience (if any). If you are a first-timer, specify any qualifications and/or qualities which show you to have business acumen. State the exact amount you wish to borrow and to what use it will be put.

Ideally, you should put all this in the post prior to your meeting so that the manager will have had time to digest your proposal in advance.

The fact that you have made the effort to commit your thoughts to paper demonstrates that you mean business – and this can only be to your advantage. You will be seen as a pragmatist who has considered her idea thoroughly, rather than a dilettante dabbling in dreams.

Combine this realistic approach with enthusiasm and you are at least halfway towards selling your idea and bridging this first, crucial link in the entrepreneurial chain.

If you receive a half-hearted, 'pat on the head' response, shop around for a more enlightened person with whom to do business. After all, bank managers are supposed to offer a service and if all you are getting is a put-down, take your custom elsewhere.

Maureen Foers' eight years in banking stood her in excellent stead when she began trying to raise capital for her recruitment agency on Humberside. "I appreciated what banks would want from a potential business, and a lot of information was stored away inside me that I could use," she recalls.

Between her banking career and setting up in business in 1971 there was a stint as managing executive of a small group of private employment agencies, from which she was fired. "I was too ambitious. ... After five days a week of trying to make somebody else's fortune, I thought: 'If I could do it for them, I could do it for myself'." It was the days before redundancy pay, and being sacked provided the necessary spur to action.

Three aunts loaned her £500 to get started, but when the time came to approach her bank for more working capital she encountered hurdle number one. She got short shrift from her bank manager, to whom women in business were clearly alien creatures from another planet. "Fortunately for me, but unfortunately for him, he died, and out of his misfortune a manager came from London. This manager had a very different approach to women in business and he is still extremely supportive."

Maureen's business has expanded over the years in several different directions. There have been four separate ventures. First, the staff bureau, the bedrock of Maureen's 'empire'. When unemployment began to bite in the North East, she moved into office services, inviting companies to bring their work to *her*. It was an ideal way of utilizing the talents of women who had the necessary experience but were not able to work full-time. She retrained them for nothing, updating their skills.

She then branched out into direct mail, providing specialist facilities for bulk mail and distributing companies' marketing literature. Finally, she opened a crèche for about thirty children.

Hull-born and bred, she was reasonably well-known in the city when she set up her staff agency. Now, nearly two decades on, Maureen's company has turned into the largest independent commercial training centre in the United Kingdom, with an annual turnover of half a million pounds. She defines its function as 'human resource management'. It employs about 30 staff, all women (full-time and part-time) and is based on two floors of a large old building in the centre of Hull.

She is divorced, with a daughter in her twenties who works with the elderly. Maureen's marriage broke up before she went into business and she is now her grandson's legal guardian: 'He is one reason for keeping my feet on the ground.' She describes herself as a 'reasonably good businesswoman who is also good at Lego!'

> *'I just went to a local printer's and asked them to give me credit, then down to London and tried to get advertising agencies to book into it. '*

There have been few serious stumbling blocks, and family and friends have mostly been very supportive, though some people, mainly women, were sceptical at first. Their attitude was: 'She will surely come a cropper' and they reckoned she wouldn't last three months. Maureen gleans some satisfaction from having proved them wrong.

Carey Labovitch launched her own student magazine, *Blitz*, when she was at Oxford in 1980 (reading French and Italian), with no finance and no experience of either business or corporate worlds. "I just went to a local printer's and asked them to give me credit, then down to London and tried to get advertising agencies to book into it. I did that on a quarterly basis every term, with fellow students contributing.

Blitz was designed to be a cross between what the 'pop' press and the women's magazines were offering, a magazine for a young, 'upwardly mobile' readership.

It was the height of the recession. People like myself were doing their exams and coming out afterwards and not getting jobs, however qualified they were. So a lot of my contemporaries were turning hobbies into professions – like photography, or journalism. . . .

There was a big change in the early eighties – the feeling that anyone could do anything."

Unusually perhaps, Carey never sought financial advice. "I've always been very stubborn. I felt that if I couldn't do it myself there would be no point in doing it, and so I learned the hard way.

That's why I can sit back quite arrogantly now and say: 'I do know about that, I've *been* there', and can actually command other people. In the beginning I sold advertising on all the magazines because I couldn't afford to take on staff. I used to go into agencies and I was just Carey from *Blitz*, not Carey Labovitch, the publisher.

One guy said: 'Very glossy, very nice magazine, Where's the money coming from?' I said: 'Well, the money is purely people like you who give me advertising against credit from printers', and he wouldn't believe me until I showed him my cheque card with my signature and pointed out my name in a magazine. . . .

I was young, I had no experience and people could see right through that, so I had to bullshit my way through everything."

The real boost came when, after issue three, *Blitz* won the Guardian's Best Graphics award, which means instant recognition from the wholesalers, "and so by the time I left Oxford in 1983 I already had a magazine that was distributed all over the UK. It seemed logical to go on with that rather than join a milk round."

Having survived initially on her college grant, Carey then went in search of London offices and tried to persuade banks to give her an overdraft to start the magazine professionally. For four years she drew no salary, just lived off petty cash.

She looked after all the advertising, paste-up and editorial, in conjunction with her partner, Simon Tesler. A fellow student, he is now managing editor of *Blitz*, a co-director and also Carey's live-in partner. They set up the company together when they left Oxford. "Having someone to lean on in that respect has been a great help."

Their roles are clearly defined. Carey has borne most of the financial burdens, while Tesler has shouldered the creative ones.

For most women entrepreneurs, the biggest obstacle is finance. You might be a free spirit in terms of the type of business you choose and your style of leadership, but you are very much at the mercy of market forces. The success, or otherwise, of your enterprise will depend not only on the benevolence of your bank manager but also on a volatile bank interest rate, which is totally outside your control.

You may be working on a shoestring and a soaring bank rate can soon decimate your cash flow.

Then there is the perennial problem of late (or non) payers.

> *'You have met your deadline and you suddenly find that payment is not forthcoming. Bills start to pile up on your desk, making you feel depressed and vulnerable.'*

You have completed an order on time and at breakneck speed. You have met your deadline and you suddenly find that payment is not forthcoming. Bills start to pile up on your desk, making you feel depressed and vulnerable.

Unlike Carey Labovitch, many women in business prefer to leave the financial side to husbands or male acquaintances. Sometimes, men are deliberately taken on as business partners in order to give business advice or negotiate credit.

Fashion designer **Betty Jackson** launched her company in 1981, with her French husband and business partner, David. David looks after company finances, leaving Betty free to concentrate on the creative side.

"I'm terribly interested in the financial side, but the doing of it bores me to death," she admits, candidly. "I want to be able to say: 'Right, we'll do a cash flow and a budget and I want to see it by the end of the week'. Now, I can have people to do that whereas, before, I had to do it myself."

Initially, David put in the main share of the money, Betty contributed a small amount and they raised the rest via a bank loan set against orders.

The first couple of meetings with their bank manager touched on all-too-familiar ground. "He thought I wasn't involved in the money at all and started directing conversation at my husband, . . . but I think I probably have enough personality to overcome that sort of thing!"

The situation was eased by David's limited knowledge of English – "and so at that stage I was translating conversations as well. I began to answer questions and interrupt, just to let the manager know that, although everything was to be a joint decision, *I* was very much fifty per cent of that joint decision and ideas came from both of us."

In terms of overall direction and strategy of the company, their roles do overlap. "We very rarely get the chance to talk about things together during working hours because there are so many other people we have to talk to, and so strategy decisions are often taken at home."

David has introduced all the latest computerized accounting systems, "which have organized us incredibly well . . . I know that I would have been reticent about doing that, but he did it and it's terribly efficient. It means *we* are efficient, too."

She had originally wanted to be a sculptor, but found she

was allergic to all the things that sculptors have to use. . . . "It's like being too tall to be a ballet dancer!" There was "no burning ambition to be a clothes designer since I was four." She was an illustrator and sort of *happened* into fabrics and textiles.

Susi Madron's Manchester-based company, 'Cycling for Softies' began almost accidentally, after a family holiday in France in 1980.

"It originated from my buying a bicycle to take my five-

> — '*He thought I wasn't involved in the money at all and started directing conversation at my husband . . .* ' —

year-old daughter to school. We put a child's seat on the back. My husband had also just bought a bike. And when it came to 'What shall we do for a holiday this year?', I said: 'Why not take the bikes over to France?'

I know France well, having lived in Paris. . . . We bought a 72-hour return ticket to Dieppe. We thought if we discovered at Dieppe that the hills were too much for us we could get on the next ferry back but, having got up the hills, we decided to carry on.

It took us 2½ weeks. We went down the back lanes and stayed in places for a couple of days, then whizzed on to the next place."

Her husband, Roy, was at Manchester Business School and was waiting for funding for several research projects. His research came up trumps and he spent three years funding the business while their house was up as collateral.

Their bank manager had been supportive during the first

year, but his head office took one look at their figures and said 'No go'. After that, they sought the services of a financial adviser who specialized in obtaining government loans for small businesses. He suggested sources of finance and they traipsed around the city's banks, putting their proposal to the manager of every bank in Manchester.

Eventually, they struck lucky and secured a loan of £18,000, which they used to set up the 1983 season.

Meanwhile, Roy's business contacts had asked if they could use the venture as an example for one of their banking courses. "They came and looked at our figures for the first couple of years and said: 'We'll report back'. . . .

Most of the people on the course were bank managers, and having done a report on our activities, they said: 'Basically, this company should close down'. By that time, we were into our third year and making a profit, so it didn't matter! . . . but we had had exactly the same response from banks as well. One or two managers thought it was a super *idea*, but banks don't trade on good ideas. They trade in figures and you have to be seen to have a success by the end of 12 months."

— '*One* or two managers thought it was a super idea, but banks don't trade on good ideas. They trade in figures and you have to be seen to have a success by the end of 12 months. —,

From an office in their back bedroom Susi Madron's business has now moved into the city centre, with eight full-time staff. Two more are based in each of the company's areas in France, plus three itinerant supervisors.

Apart from her penchant for all things French, Susi had never worked in the travel industry before. She was a housewife whose only experience of being a boss was running a small citizens' advice bureau in Hebden Bridge, Yorkshire (annual stipend: £1,000).

She has two prime rules for success:

Funding

Have somebody to help you fund the business when you start out. Make sure you have enough working capital to see you through the early, leaner times, bearing in mind that it could be up to five years before you begin to reap the benefits.

Marketing

Work out, as far as possible, who your customer is before you begin. "We'd decided our customer was like *us* because we had had that experience and enjoyed it, and therefore we said: 'Can we get a lot more of *us*?' That was our basis."

Before leaping into the unknown, it's wise to test the water first. Having chosen your area of interest, work at it in your spare time for a while. Break yourself gently into the idea of entrepreneurship. And don't be put off by well-meaning (or otherwise) friends or relatives who tell you you need your head examined. This type of response often stems from envy: the fact that you happen to have had an idea which *they* wish they had dreamed up and had the courage to put into practice.

So – dare to be different, but sound out the situation beforehand.

Betty Jackson believes that previous experience in one's chosen field is vital. She receives numerous letters from women saying: 'I want to start up my own business. I make clothes for friends and think I'd be really good'.

"I really do discourage people like that, because I don't think it does the fashion industry – or them – any good at all. It's the idea that you just make a few frocks, hang them on a rail and think you design clothes. There are so many things involved: the costing, the shipping instructions, the selling. . . .

If people are going to spend money buying your product you have to provide that service to the best possible measure and I don't believe that anybody who does it on a domestic scale can do that.

I think that internationally we in Britain are regarded very much as a cottage industry. The British have a problem in that success is a dirty word – you know, you can't be seen to be too successful, and if you are, then it's all rather *nasty* and not spoken about, which is ridiculous.

It's the reverse in America – in Italy and France, too . . . but in Britain it's 'you've become too commercial' or whatever, and until we get *that* right. . . . Plus: I think British fashion designers are very bad at putting themselves across. That is all related to low budgets and not having excess cash.

I think as well, since about 1982, we've been victims of a movement that was so keen on London and did anything to buy British, and that bubble has definitely burst."

Between leaving Birmingham College of Art and Design and launching her business, Betty spent around eight years exploring different aspects of the fashion world – "getting to know how the structure of the industry works, because I believe that it's foolish to go into something unless you know exactly what you are doing."

Her advice is: choose your company and make them employ you. Go and observe, glean information, learn their methods – and be enthusiastic.

"A designer has to be all things to all people. At the end of the day it's deliveries, being on time, having the right quality and filling a market area that is important."

Most of the time she manages to balance creative and administrative duties reasonably well. She admits there is a danger of the latter taking over. "You can get completely bogged down with it, but then I have a workroom with pattern cutters and machinists who require work and ideas from *me*. . . . We do the show and the next *day* I am buying fabrics for the next collection, so it is a continual process and one gets into the swing of it.

It would be horrible to have days when there's nothing to do."

The sheer energy and resourcefulness of all my interviewees will ensure they will never be idle. It is not in their natures to sit back and wait for work to come to them. Even the most successful of entrepreneurs cannot afford the luxury of complacency.

— *'I think that internationally we in Britain are regarded very much as a cottage industry. The British have a problem in that success is a dirty word . . .'* —

Making it as a fashion designer is a lot more hard graft than glamour. So, too, is editing a magazine for the youth market.

Carey Labovitch: "Publishing looks glamorous from the outside: glossy magazine, beautiful people – but it's just like working in a normal office, only with longer hours and frantic deadlines."

Her advice? "You should try and develop a very strong character. It's all about selling yourself. So many people want to get into magazine publishing and you really have to be motivated."

Like Betty Jackson, she gets stacks of letters. Visits, too – from budding editors, many of them undergraduates, wanting to pick her brains about starting a magazine. Too many, she finds, have wonderful ideas and don't think them through.

One woman whose germ of an idea has snowballed into a small multinational is ***Steve Shirley***, Managing Director of the largest independent computer software house – F International – in the United Kingdom. It offers a huge range of highly sophisticated, cost-effective computing services, with a 1987 turnover of £10 million, and growing in excess of the industry average.

What makes it unique is its flexibility: the ethos behind F International (historically, F = Freelance) is the freedom of its workers to fit their hours around their lifestyle. The company deploys a workforce of around a thousand. Many work from home, using a network of personal computers provided, insured and maintained by the company. Unlike most traditional home workers they are highly paid: "High fees for people with rare skills", is how Steve Shirley see its.

"Probably one of the secrets of our corporate success," she says, "is that we have tapped an access to a labour market which is in very short supply worldwide." Company policy is to use the services of people who are, because of dependents, unable to work in a 9 to 5 office set-up. The company's Mission, enshrined in its Charter, is to use "modern telecommunications to develop the intellectual energy of people who cannot work in a conventional environment."

As such, it is ideal for women, enabling them to combine work and motherhood without having to drop out of the job market for several years to bring up a family. Steve Shirley deplores the crying waste of women's skills caused by this enforced career gap. "Women should be able to choose to spend time with their children without sacrifice of career or self in the process."

Much time and money is spent on in-house training and re-training as workers' skills are continually updated in line with the needs of a rapidly changing industry. Steve Shirley reckons that if a person stops learning they would be unemployable within three years.

She launched her company in 1962, with £6 and no previous business experience. She was not, however, new to the hi-tech world, having carved out a steady career as a computer technician. But with a small son to look after, she began to reap the advantages of going freelance.

"The industry saw me as a crank, but I was too busy to take

a great deal of notice," she recalls lightheartedly.

She was awarded an OBE for her services to the computer industry, and from her initial small team of associated programmers, the company has swelled its ranks to include consultants and analysts, designers and technical writers.

More than a hundred staff have received ten-year service awards, and a few have reached the 20-year mark, which entitles them to membership of a club.

> *'The company's Mission, enshrined in its Charter, is to use "modern telecommunications to develop the intellectual energy of people who cannot work in a conventional environment."'*

F International operates from modest headquarters in Berkhamsted, Herts., but its scale of operation extends throughout Northern Europe.

The company is constantly covering new ground such as marketing orientation and assertiveness training. "We see training as a strategic investment," claims Steve Shirley. More and more of her colleagues are becoming managers. All the company's line managers are women.

Because the computer industry is moving so fast, Steve Shirley concentrates these days on the managerial (not technical) side of things. She thinks of herself as an entrepreneurial manager. "One characteristic of entrepreneurs is that we seem to be able to pursue several goals simultaneously, compared with professional managers with skills I really admire but who achieve in only one sphere at a time.

Many women just don't realize what it costs to pursue a professional management career in a corporate environment and they see the external trappings of success without seeing the cost."

Whatever career choices you make, some personal sacrifice is necessary. In Steve Shirley's case, it has been her social life: dinner parties and holidays have had to go, but not family life, which is very important to her. Her husband has been supportive throughout: "I don't think one can do anything so eccentric unless one's marriage is pretty sound."

She sums up what, for her, is the ultimate reason for her success. "I am interested in achievement, not power. This is a new, federated style of business which has proved successful and allows me to work with teams of very highly motivated people. It's become my way of life."

> *'This is a new, federated style of business which has proved successful and allows me to work teams of very highly motivated people.'*

Along with Anita Roddick and her Body Shop International, Debbie Moore's Pineapple Dance Studios and Pru Leith's catering and restaurant venture, Steve Shirley is an admirable role model. She epitomizes all that is best about entrepreneurship: gritty determination, enthusiasm, a readiness to adapt to changing trends.

In a Nuffield Foundation survey of fifty London-based female entrepreneurs in 1982,[46] most were motivated by a combination of desire for financial success and personal freedom. Their ages ranged from 26 to 71 and their businesses covered a broad spectrum, from modest, home-based concerns to international organizations with several hundred employees.

The women's definition of freedom included freedom from male hierarchies as well as from the subordination of being an employee. For some, running a business was a way of outclassing men on male terms. As one woman said: "I'm in a man's business because I want to prove I'm as good as they are. In fact, I want to prove I'm better. . . . I've been dominated by men, so I just enjoy achieving the things men want to achieve – and doing it better than them."

At the same time, these women were worried about losing their femininity and acquiring the kind of ruthlessness and aggression normally associated with men.

Maureen Foers: "A lot of people would probably say that in business you have to be ruthless. I would disagree. 'Ruthless' infers (sic) that you would do whatever it takes regardless of the cost and consequences for yourself or anybody else. I prefer to say: 'I will succeed regardless of the many setbacks'.

Initially, I was in a recognized women's world of business: the employment agency world. This was considered more acceptable. Now, I compete with men all the time. I have probably grown a very thick skin."

Any male client who behaves in a sexist way towards Maureen is underestimating her: "He is giving me a big advantage, a head start, because I am *not* 'the little woman in the corner' . . . I hope I have developed a certain amount of role play so that I can move back from the situation. . . ."

Rather than act tough, Maureen practises some of her negotiating skills. "I like to think I am a good negotiator. I smile readily. . . . Within my company budget there is always money for my personal self-development." She keeps up with the latest courses on assertiveness and leadership, and feels she can never learn too much.

She belongs to endless committees. "I have had the token woman role so often I ought to be branded with it! . . . The more I work, the more I thrive on it. I am very much a workaholic."

When she 'outgrows' a particular committee she moves on to another. "My needs change. . . . My weakness is that I am probably overcommitted – but I am a delegator, not an abdicator. I now have a staff of thirty, so my delegating can't be too bad!

Probably one reason I am such a dedicated businesswoman is that I failed in marriage. I would hate to fail in business as well."

When she married (in her early twenties) she saw her future through rose-tinted glasses. Now, in her late-forties, she would need to be sure that "the person with whom I wanted to spend my life would accept my need to be an individual. He would probably have to be a very understanding person to take me on."

The strong emotional investment and long-term commitment of entrepreneurship can wreck social and family life.

The Nuffield survey showed how the fears of some men extended to their virility. As one woman put it: "I'm a threat because I run my own business. It goes down to a very sexual level – men cannot sexually function. . . . They've been brought up to be the dominant sex, but we make them feel inadequate."

The survey showed that many women in business were not given anything like the same level of unpaid support from their husbands that their male counterparts expected *as of right* from their wives.

Some women regard their businesses as substitute children to be nurtured until ready to leave the 'home' base.

Carey Labovitch: "The magazines are like children. I gave birth to them. They are my babies. I must make sure that they grow up properly, with enough nursemaids looking after them at the office. I do feel very maternal towards them, and as a result I take my work home. I sleep work and think work."

For all the interviewees, the rewards of being their own boss far outweighed the pitfalls.

> '*The* magazines are like children. I gave birth to them. They are my babies. I must make sure that they grow up properly, with enough nursemaids looking after them at the office.*'

Maureen Foers: "I enjoy the success and I must admit I enjoy the power. The money side I am not too concerned about. As long as I have a decent car and live reasonably well with my family, I am fine.

I still have an overdraft, but with over 16 years' pedigree I am now considered a good risk.

What is nice these days is that people come to *me*. I no longer have to go out and dig for work. That, more than anything, I find very satisfying."

Betty Jackson: "This is the sort of business that grabs you by the throat and won't let go. It is so stimulating. It can take over your whole life. Probably one of the most pleasurable things in the world is if you see somebody who has been into a shop or department store and comes out wearing stuff that looks great and feels great. That's better than being on TV or getting an article in any newspaper.

All we are doing is actually *dressing* people, and then we've done our job. . . . And I love fabric, colour, texture, the whole creative process."

Susi Madron: "You get confidence in dealing with bank managers and suddenly realize you don't have to doff your cap! You can actually say to them: 'Would you come round with the Rolls and pick up the money this week?' and it gives you enormous confidence, so that side of it is very good for a woman.

> *I believe that the most important thing now is that I no longer have to battle with a male dominated society and that I am sufficiently accepted to do things my own way without apologizing, because my way has been found to be effective and successful.*

As a woman you are allowed to be emotional, so if I come across as somebody who loves what she is doing and loves the fact that other people are enjoying it, that's what they expect me to be, and so that's very helpful.

If you have a product which you think is right and you are enthusiastic about, you are able to sell it, so, in a sense, the pitfalls go away."

Steve Shirley: "I believe that the most important thing now is that I no longer have to battle with a male dominated society and that I am sufficiently accepted to do things my own way without apologizing, because my way has been found to be effective and successful. Success gives me the freedom to be accepted as a whole person."

Carey Labovitch: "My aim is to keep developing and expanding the business. I will feel happier when we have more titles and fifty or so staff working for me. I want this small publishing house to double in the next year or two so that I can feel safe that the titles will just run themselves. Then, eventually, I can go off and do something else – like interior design . . ."

WHERE TO GET HELP

Apart from your bank manager, there are other sources of initial help.

1   Your local Small Firms Centre, run by the Department of Industry (Dial 100 and ask for Freephone Enterprise).

2   Enterprise agencies. There are now around 300 of these in Britain. They are mostly run by local authorities and sponsored by large companies. They give free advice and some organize courses and seminars for anyone wanting to set up in business. One worth contacting is Jane Skinner's Women's Enterprise Development Agency (mentioned on page 176), at Aston Science Park, Love Lane, Aston Triangle, Birmingham 4.

3   Small business training courses and workshops – run by the Manpower Services Commission (MSC). For details, contact your nearest JobCentre. They may also have details of the MSC's Enterprise Allowance Scheme, which pays £40 a week for one year to supplement your business income. To be eligible you must have been on unemployment or supplementary benefit for at least eight weeks.

4 Your local Chamber of Commerce.

5 Consider taking out a franchise. This will match *your* idea with another person's resources for developing it. It accounts for more than 7,000 jobs in over 8,000 U.K. outlets. Bear in mind that it could cramp your creative style as you will be limited to selling only the products and services of the franchise company. Scour the small print of the contract for possible loopholes, and get it checked by a solicitor and accountant before signing on the dotted line. One of the most famous examples of the franchise technique is Anita Roddick's Body Shop venture, now a national mini-empire.

While you get established, and before you complete the changeover from employee to self-employed, you will need a few basic tools to set you up:

a an efficient answering machine. There are some good, simple, cheap ones on the market. Renting is a false economy, as just one call could recoup the entire cost – and more.

b business cards: not too flash.

c headed notepaper: ditto.

d typewriter and/or word processor.

e desk and filing cabinet.

f cash book. Use one side of the page for earnings, the other side for expenses. Keep all receipts and enter them in a loose-leaf binder.

Perhaps the most important asset is a good accountant. She or he will be able to advise you on how to keep your tax bill to a minimum by claiming all the expenses incurred in running your business – for example, everyday running costs such as heating, lighting, telephone, stationery, motoring.

Strategy For Survival

HINTS WITH HINDSIGHT AND WITHOUT TEARS

I t's a cliché, but a truism nonetheless, that a woman has to sell herself twice as hard as a man to be a success. *Staying at the top* can be every bit as daunting, perhaps more so, both because of the danger of slipping into complacency, of losing that competitive *edge* once the main battle is over, and also a sense that, as a woman, you are permanently on trial and having to prove you are up to the job.

At meetings or large gatherings you will almost inevitably be outnumbered by men. Because of your high visibility people will remember your name. They will also notice and remember any mistakes you make. The higher you climb, the harder you tumble – and the harder it is simply to relax and let events carry you along.

Jane Reed recalls someone once saying to her, when she was much further down the ladder: 'You're made for Life – you're *there*'. "I said: 'Nobody is ever *there*', and it was never truer. The higher you go the easier it is to fall."

There is also the difficulty of maintaining the same level of energy and enthusiasm after the initial flush of excitement has begun to fade.

However, proven success earns you the respect that fuels the confidence that you need to consolidate your position. As **Linda Agran** puts it, "Having a track record is quite wonderful. Now, if I open my mouth, people assume that I know what I'm talking about and it adds enormous weight. I can talk about Einstein's Theory of Relativity which I know b-all about, but people think: 'Well, she must know, because she's done all that. . . .'"

It's getting accepted in the first place that is the tricky bit, as my interviewees will testify. In the Institute of Directors' 1985 survey into 'What it takes to get there', the main obstacles pinpointed were male prejudice, old boy networks and motherhood. Nobody ever gave up power without a struggle and men are unlikely to want to change a system that keeps them in power, a system that (on the whole) does not make it easy for the other half of the population to be high achievers.

Job-sharing, flexible hours and the proliferation of women's networks all go some way towards redressing the balance. In the end, though, it is down to *you*: to your ability, determination and will to succeed. Without those basic attributes, you won't even get past first base.

Here, from my contributors, is a pot-pourri of hints for survival culled from the wisdom of many years and contrasting professions. Some of it is mildly conflicting. All of it is eminently sensible. Collectively, it should set you thinking.

1 Be yourself.
2 Choose carefully who you work for. If it's a man, choose one who is pro-women and wants to see you get on.
3 Find a female ally and/or mentor.
4 Find some male allies, too.
5 Join an expanding company in an expanding industry.
6 Experiment at first. If you are not sure which direction to take, look around and find out as much as you can about the areas of work which most appeal to you. Take your time. Better to

explore the options early on than make a hasty and wrong first choice.

7 If exams are necessary, take them and pass them as quickly as you can. These days, any extra qualifications are almost bound to enhance your career chances.

8 Grasp the opportunities as and when they occur – and, whatever you do, *don't let anyone put you off*. Don't be deterred by people who think they know what is best for you. Sometimes they do, but usually they don't. Listen to advice, but make your own decision.

9 Set yourself goals. Ask yourself: 'Where do I want to be in one/five/ten years' time?'

10 Keep away from office politics.

11 Believe in yourself. Be confident without false modesty, and self-critical without self-doubt.

12 Try not to over-react to criticism, or always to attribute it to your gender ('So-and-so is only picking on me because I'm a woman'). Learn the art of resilience and don't be put off when the going gets tough.

13 If you are contemplating joining an organization, look to see where the most senior woman is. If there isn't one, then you might be fighting a losing battle.

14 See yourself as a *whole* person. Always be aware of the parts that are incomplete and don't neglect these – develop them. Work out the kind of lifestyle that is right for *you*. What about children? How much time off will you need/want while they are growing up? However engrossing your job may be, don't let it become an obsession. Give yourself permission to relax and explore other avenues.

15 Do your best, but don't be content with second-rate. Reach for the stars. You can always fall on the roof.

USEFUL ADDRESSES

**The Association of
Women Solicitors**
8 Bream's Buildings,
London EC4A 1HP

**British Institute of
Management (BIM)**
Management House,
Cottingham Road,
Corby,
Northants NN17 1TT

City Women's Network
20 Essex Street,
London WC2R 3AL

The Pepperell Unit
(They run a variety of
courses and workshops for
women aimed at enhancing
women's talents and self-
development)
The Industrial Society,
Robert Hyde House,
48 Bryanston Square,
London W1H 7LN

Network
(The Association for
Women in the Professions,
Commerce, Industry and
the Arts),
25 Park Road,
London NW1 6XN

The 300 Group
(A non-party group formed
in 1980 to seek the equal
representation of women in
Parliament, and to
encourage and train women
to seek and hold public and
political office. Many active
regional groups)
9 Poland Street,
London W1V 3DG

Women in Enterprise
(An organization set up in
1986. Its aims are to provide
information for aspiring
female entrepreneurs or
small businesswomen, on
finance and sources of
advice, and to develop and
promote training
programmes, also to
influence educational
establishments, business
schools and enterprise
agencies, persuading them
to look at running a business
from a woman's point of
view as well as a man's.
Baroness Seear is WE's
Chief Patron)
26 Bond Street,
Wakefield WF1 2QP

Women in Management (WIM)

(Publishes three newsletters
a year, and periodically
holds major events, regular
discussion evenings and
executive lunches for senior
women)
64 Marryatt Road,
London SW19 5BN

Equal Opportunities Commission

(They will supply lists of
courses aimed at women)
Overseas House,
Quay Street,
Manchester

Manpower Services Commission

(They provide lists of
contact groups and courses
for women trainees)
Head Office
Moorfoot 1
Sheffield S1 4PQ

Small Business Bureau

(National Co-ordinator:
Irene Jeffery)
32 Smith Square,
London SW1P 3HH

SOURCES

1   Janice LaRouche & Regina Ryan, 'Strategies for Women at Work' (Unwin, 1985)

2   Peter Brock, 'How a Well Educated Wife Can Give You Heart Disease' (Guardian: 7.12.83)

3   Christine Tongue, 'Why a lot of Directors are Impostors' (Guardian: 21.8.86)

4   David Gaister, 'All Managers under the Skin' (Women in Management Review Vol. 2, No. 3 – Autumn '86)

5   London Standard, 15.12.86

6   Angela Phillips, 'Attacking the root causes of child abuse' (The Independent: 24.7.87)

7   Polly Toynbee, 'The Way to Parents' Lib' (Guardian: 25.8.87)

8   Penny Perrick, 'Buried Treasure in the Office' (Times: 24.6.83)

9   Alan Road, 'Rising Against Dictators' (Observer: 7.12.86)

10 Ms London magazine, 4.1.82

11 Roger Bennett, 'How Performance Appraisals hurt Women Managers' (W.I.M. Review – Autumn '86)

12 Jilly Cooper, 'How to Survive Work and Wedlock' (Methuen, 1970 – pp. 28–29)

13 Natasha Josefowitz, 'Paths to Power' (Columbus Books, 1987)

14 John Nicholson, 'Habits' (Pan, 1978)

15 ibid

16 John Nicholson, 'Men And Women (How Different Are They?)' (O.U.P. 1984, p. 119)

17 Mary Kay Ash, 'On People Management' (Macdonald, 1984, p. 23)

18 ibid, p. 37

19 Natasha Josefowitz, 'Paths to Power' (Columbus Books, 1987)

20 Jenny Woolf, 'When Power is Par for the Female Course' (The Independent: 23.3.87)

21 'So You Think You Can Manage?' (A Video Arts Guide – Methuen, 1984), p. 43

22 Angela Neustatter, 'Defence Tactics' (Guardian: 13.3.85)

23 'Women and Men – Building Bridges' (Everywoman, February 1987)

24 Bryan Nicholson, Women on the Board conference (24.10.86)

25 Margaret Horsefield, 'Today's Top Woman' (Observer: 9.3.86)

26 Nick Higham, 'BBC Women – Opportunity Knocks?' (Broadcast: 3.4.87)

27 Ann Kent, 'Women under Pressure' (Times: 29.5.85)

28 Rosemary Burr, 'Female Tycoons' (Rosters)

29 Ann Kent, 'Women under Pressure' (Times: 29.5.85)

30 Martin Wainwright, 'Fun and war games for all of the company's men' (Guardian: 31.3.87)

31 'Stressing Pressures' (Times: 12.8.87)

32 Liz Gill, 'A Week in Paradise is a Long Time' (Times: 27.4.87)

33 Ann Sedley & Melissa Benn, 'Sexual Harassment at Work' (NCCL, 1982)

34 ibid

35 Over 21 (May 1987)

36 Sedley & Benn, 'Sexual Harassment at Work' (NCCL, 1982)

37 ibid

38 Suzanne Lowry, 'At work on sex and sexism' (Sunday Times: 28.8.83)

39 M.S.C. Chairman Bryan Nicholson, Women on the Board conference (24.10.86)

40 Sedley & Benn, 'Sexual Harassment at Work' (NCCL, 1982)

41 Pat Garratt, 'Sexual Power Games in the Office' (Times: 30.7.86)

42 Sedley & Benn, 'Sexual Harassment' in the Office (NCCL, 1982)

43 Pat Garratt, 'Sexual Power Games in the Office' (Times: 30.7.86)

44 Carmel Fitzsimons, 'How Women can stand and fight sexual harassment' (Observer: 7.9.86)

45 Jane Skinner, 'Enter the Entrepreneuse' (W.I.M. Review, Autumn 1986)

46 Nuffield Foundation funded survey of entrepreneurship among women caried out by New Society (issue 6.9.82)